CONVERSATION PIECE

Also by NOEL COWARD

CAVALCADE
DESIGN FOR LIVING
PRIVATE LIVES
POST MORTEM

CONVERSATION PIECE

A Romantic Comedy

by

NOEL COWARD

London
WILLIAM HEINEMANN LTD

FIRST PUBLISHED 1934

———

PRINTED IN GREAT BRITAIN
AT THE WINDMILL PRESS, KINGSWOOD, SURREY

To
G. E. CALTHROP
This Play is Gratefully and Affectionately
Dedicated

This play was first produced at His Majesty's Theatre on Friday, February 16th, 1934, with the following cast (in order of appearance):

SOPHIE OTFORD	.. ..	Heather Thatcher
MARTHA JAMES	.. ..	Moya Nugent
MRS. DRAGON	.. ..	Betty Shale
PAUL, DUC DE CHAUCIGNY-VARENNES	.. ..	Noel Coward
MELANIE	.. ..	Yvonne Printemps
ROSE (Her Maid)	.. ..	Maidie Andrews
THE MARQUIS OF SHEERE	..	Louis Hayward
THE EARL OF HARRINGFORD		George Sanders
LORD BRACEWORTH ⎫ Regency		Pat Worsley
LORD DOYNING ⎬ Rakes		Antony Brian
MR. HAILSHAM ⎭		Sidney Grammer
THE DUCHESS OF BENEDEN		Winifred Davis
THE DUKE OF BENEDEN	..	Athole Stewart
LADY JULIA CHARTERIS	..	Irene Browne
HANNAH (Her Maid)	..	Elizabeth Corcoran
A TIGER	.. ..	Tommy Hayes
MISS GOSLETT	.. ..	Everley Gregg
MISS MENTION	.. ..	Molly Lumley
LORD KENYON	.. ..	Penryn Bannerman
LORD ST. MARYS	.. ..	Kim Peacock
FISHERMEN	.. ..	Reginald Thurgood William McGuigan Evan Jones Roy Hall
COUNTESS OF HARRINGFORD		Sheila Pattrick
LADY BRACEWORTH	.. ..	Betty Elburn

MRS. HAILSHAM	.. ..	Winifred Campbell
HON. JULIAN KANE	.. ..	St. John Lauri
MR. AMOS	.. ..	Alex Robertson
BUTLER	.. ..	Claude Farrow
MR. JONES	.. ..	Leonard Michel
COURTESAN	.. ..	Jean Barnes

SOLDIERS, GUESTS, etc. ..
{
Albert Dudley
Ronald Pope
Geoffrey Brighton
Esmond Wilding
}

MILLINERS, LADIES OF THE TOWN, VISITORS, etc. ..
{
Maysie Andrews
Jean Beckworth
Dorothy Drover
Grace Gorrod
Valerie Hobson
Vivienne Maurice
Beryl Norman
Enid Settle
June Spencer-Dyke
Marcelle Turner
Winifred Talbot
}

CHILDREN .. ..
{
John Jaques
Henry Bryce
Ryall Corderey
Lydia Craddock
Constance Bowdler
Betty Parker
Celia White
}

The whole of the action of the play occurs at Brighton, 1811.

CONVERSATION PIECE

ACT I

Scene 1

PROLOGUE

*At the end of the Overture, the Curtain rises disclosing a
painted curtain, which depicts, in pastel colours, the
Brighton of the Regency.*

*SOPHIE, MARTHA and DRAGON come in, exquisitely
dressed in the fashion of 1811, and each carrying a little
mask on an ivory stick. They stand, formally, side by
side, with their masks held before their eyes. They
lower them in order to speak, and retire behind them
again when they are silent.*

BOTH : Ladies and Gentlemen.

SOPHIE : A Prologue to a play is out of date,
      A leisurely technique of past decades,
      So please regard us as two friendly shades
      Returning down the years to indicate,
      More by our presence, than by what we say,
      The atmosphere and tempo of this play.

MARTHA : My friend has explained it most concisely,
      She always was one to put things nicely!

SOPHIE : We represent the fine but faded flower
      Of that old " Demi Monde " that used to be
      At Vauxhall, and at Brighton by the sea
      Before the pure in heart came into power,
      Before a great, but sanctimonious Queen
      Firmly rang down the curtain on our scene.

MARTHA : Please don't suppose *our* flowers were
    faded,
    Others were pushed, *we* were persuaded!
SOPHIE : The interruptions of my friend are meant
    To clarify for you our "Status Quo"
    A social level neither high nor low
    With which we were entirely content
    And which provides the background, may I say,
    Of this polite, but faintly raffish play.
    *To music, and with great dignity, they part the
curtains on the first scene.*

ACT I

SCENE II

The Scene is part of the Parade at Brighton. There is a railing running the whole length of the stage and, behind it, a row of demure Georgian houses. There is room only for pedestrians to pass between the railing and the houses.

When the curtain rises it is about eleven o'clock on a sunny spring morning. There are two FISHERMEN leaning against the railing with expressions of static resignation. Several people pass and re-pass along the Parade. Two SOLDIERS in scarlet coats stop and talk to a neat little milliner's assistant with a hat box. A LITTLE BOY runs across bowling a hoop, and two LITTLE GIRLS walk along sedately with their NURSE. The whole picture seems fresh and gay and alive, and the orchestra, which plays continually throughout the scene, celebrates the entrance of any particular character with a pleasant little burst of individual melody. Finally, SOPHIE OTFORD and MARTHA JAMES walk on from the left. They are both pretty, and charmingly dressed, and a certain manner and quality about them suggest that they are of the superior courtesan class. They walk languidly and chatter with a vivacity that one cannot help feeling is just a trifle artificial. PAUL, the Duc de Chaucigny-Varennes, enters from the right. He is a superbly dressed, neat little man of about forty-five. He appears to exude an aroma of perfection.

3

His gestures possess an authentic grace, and although they are precise they are not in the least overdone.   He turns to the front door of MELANIE'S *house and rat-tat-tats briskly on the knocker as the lights fade.*

ACT I

SCENE III

The Scene is the interior of MELANIE'S *house, to be exact, the living-room. It is charmingly furnished, and the windows at the back open on to a small balcony which looks out over the Parade and the sea. There are two doors. The one up stage right leads into a little hall and to the rest of the house. The one opposite to it up stage left leads to* MELANIE'S *bedroom.*

As the lights rise on the scene the rat-tat-tat of the knocker can be heard. This rat-tat-tat theme being a motif in the music which recurs throughout the play. The music continues, and ROSE *enters. She is* MELANIE'S *English maid, a pretty girl in the twenties. She casts a careful glance over the room to see that everything is tidy, and then runs downstairs to open the front door. After a moment she follows* PAUL *into the room. He walks in with an air of complete authority and hands her his hat, gloves, and cane.*

PAUL : Chocolate ?

ROSE : All ready, sir.

PAUL : No lumps in it ?

ROSE : Not one, sir.

PAUL : Good.

He goes over to the desk, and, placing some glasses upon his nose, seats himself at it. In a methodical business-like manner he looks through a pile of bills and

5   B

papers. ROSE *goes out to fetch the chocolate. She returns in a moment with a neatly arranged tray which she places on the desk.*

ROSE : You're sure you wouldn't like an egg, sir ?

PAUL : Quite sure, thank you.

ROSE : Nor a nice crisp bit of bacon?

PAUL : It would kill me.

ROSE : I see, sir.

PAUL (*pouring himself some chocolate*) : How is Mademoiselle ?

ROSE : Gay as a lark, sir.

PAUL : Good. How is her English this morning ?

ROSE : I don't know, sir, but my French is improving by leaps and bounds.

PAUL : Then consider yourself dismissed.

ROSE : You don't really mean that, do you, sir ?

PAUL : No.

ROSE : I didn't think you did really, sir.

PAUL : But I am very displeased with you. The rule of the house is that no one must speak French to Mademoiselle under any circumstances.

ROSE : I only said " Mon Dieu " when I dropped the nail file.

PAUL : Stick to " My God," it's more blasphemous and far more expressive.

ROSE : Very well, sir.

PAUL : This butcher's bill seems very high.

ROSE : It's the veal, I expect. Mademoiselle dearly loves a bit of veal, and I keep telling her it's unreliable.

PAUL : It isn't its integrity I question, but its cost.

ROSE : Yes, sir.

PAUL : In future no more veal except on special occasions. (*He holds out a bill.*) What does this mean ?

6

ROSE : Humbugs, sir.

PAUL : What are they ?

ROSE : Sort of big bull's eyes.

PAUL (*horrified*): Bull's eyes ?

ROSE (*laughing*): Oh, not real ones, sir, they're sweets. You tuck one in your cheek and it keeps you going for hours.

PAUL : Disgusting.

ROSE : Mademoiselle's very partial to them, sir. She saw some in a shop a long time ago, and since then we've 'ad 'em regular.

PAUL : That will be all for the moment, Rose.

ROSE (*curtseying*): Thank you, sir.

> *She goes out right.* PAUL *continues to check the accounts. After a moment* MELANIE *comes out of her bedroom. She is wearing a négligée and looks radiant, but her face is slightly distorted by an obvious bulge in the left cheek.* PAUL *springs to his feet and bows.*

PAUL : Good morning, Melanie.

MELANIE (*indistinctly*): My God !

PAUL : What's the matter ?

MELANIE (*gracefully disposing of the humbug in a small handkerchief*): Mon cher, personne ne m'a dit que——

PAUL (*sternly*): Anglais.

MELANIE (*demurely*): I did not know you were here.

PAUL : What were you eating ?

MELANIE : A 'oomboog. Tu veux le voir ?

PAUL : Non. No, certainly not.

MELANIE : They are delicious. Good morning.

PAUL : You slept well ?

MELANIE : Oui.

PAUL : Yes.

MELANIE : Yes, Paul.

7

PAUL : You have been speaking French to Rose.

MELANIE : Only a little.

PAUL : You have also been eating too much veal. I am very angry with you.

MELANIE : Please, I am sorry.

PAUL : Veal is unreliable and expensive. Those dreadful sweets are bad for your skin, and unless you learn English quickly we shall have to go away, just as we came, without money, without position, without anything.

MELANIE : Ah, ne sois pas fâché, mon cher, it is so difficult, when I awake the morning comes in at the window and makes me gay and I wish to talk very quick to Rose and say how the waves of the sea are pretty and how the sun shines and I learn better every day, I promise I do, but at the very beginning my brain does not wake itself enough and I cannot wait to find the stupid English words.

PAUL : It is so important.   So very, very important.

MELANIE : Oui, je sais bien c'est important, mais——

PAUL : Anglais.

MELANIE : Zut !   Je ne peux pas.

PAUL : You must.

MELANIE : Please do not be angry with me this morning. It is my birthday.

PAUL : Again ?

MELANIE : Well, it feels like my birthday.

PAUL : You mean that you feel particularly happy ?

MELANIE : Oui—yes.

PAUL : Why ?

MELANIE : Je ne sais pas.

PAUL : You feel happy to-day without reason, just as yesterday you felt miserable without reason.

8

You are a creature entirely lacking in balance.

MELANIE : I was an acrobat once.

PAUL : Kindly remember that you are my ward, the daughter of my dear friend the Marquis de Tramont, and that you have never even seen an acrobat, let alone been one.

MELANIE : Allez Oop ! (*She performs an acrobat's pose.*)

PAUL : Melanie !

MELANIE : Oh, comme vous êtes fastueux ce matin. Je parie que c'est encore à cause de votre foie.

PAUL : Mon foie est en parfaite santé.

MELANIE : Alors ! Pourquoi cet air de bravache ? C'est affolant. Vous m'accusez d'être heureuse sans raison, mais vous, mon ami, vous êtes âpre et désagréable également sans raison.

PAUL : Vous me désespérez.

MELANIE : Pourquoi ?

PAUL : J'insiste que vous parliez en anglais.

MELANIE : Je ne peux pas et je ne veux pas quand j'ai quelque chose d'important à dire vite, et à ce moment j'ai beaucoup à dire vite. Je travaillerai très fort. Je ferai tout ce que vous dites, mais pas quand vous êtes sévère, pas quand vous refusez de rigoler avec moi. Je vous défie !

PAUL : Soyez raisonnable, ma chère. (*He goes to her, pleading.*)

MELANIE : Riez ! Allez riez !

PAUL : Non.

MELANIE : Allons, un tout petit peu. Allez-y pour me faire plaisir.

PAUL : J'ai dis non.

MELANIE : Bon. Je ne parlerai pas un mot d'anglais

jusqu'à ce que vous souriez.   (*She sits with decision.*)

PAUL (*without mirth*) : Ha, ha, ha !

MELANIE : That is better.

PAUL : How can I make you realise that Life is serious ?

MELANIE : Because it is not serious.

PAUL : Look at these bills.

MELANIE : I see them.

PAUL : We have been here a month.

MELANIE : Yes, Paul.

PAUL : Nothing has happened at all.

MELANIE (*she rises and walks away*) : We have enough money for three months.

PAUL : Not at this rate.

MELANIE (*turning on him*) : What would you have me do ?   Have no food, have no clothes ?   Go out into the street in rags and say " Marry me.   Marry me " to every man I see ?

PAUL : Don't be ridiculous.

MELANIE : Listen. I will be sensible, even in English I will try to be sensible, but you must not ask me to be serious.   This adventure must be gay and funny.   We will cheat and lie and pretend to everyone because that is agreed, but there must be truth between us, ourselves.

PAUL (*smiling*) : Entendu !

She indicates the sofa.   He sits at the end.

MELANIE : Have you ever had a dear friend called the Marquis de Tramont ?

PAUL : No.

MELANIE : Did he ever have a daughter ?

PAUL : No.

MELANIE : Did you ever by chance visit a café called Le Petit Girondin ?

PAUL : Oui.

MELANIE : Anglais !

PAUL : Yes.

MELANIE : It was very dirty, and there was sand on the floor, and men got drunk and spat on to the sand, sometimes they were sick——

PAUL (*sharply*) : That is enough.

MELANIE : And there was a girl who sang and danced and made acrobatics like this—— (*She does a trick.*) Do you remember ?

PAUL (*admonishing*) : Melanie ! I remember an old grey château with a walled garden, and a sweet fair-haired little girl feeding the swans——

MELANIE : Liar !

PAUL : And there was peace inside the garden, and memories of much happiness, but outside the walls there was horror and bloodshed and revolution, and presently the walls crumbled and the father and mother of the little girl were led away to die——

MELANIE : Stop, please. That is too near your own truth. It has nothing to do with mine.

PAUL : If you insist on truth you shall have it. (*He firmly places her on the sofa.*) You are uneducated, illiterate, a child of the gutter, aren't you ?

MELANIE : Yes.

PAUL : Penniless ?

MELANIE : Yes.

PAUL : I am a ci-devant aristocrat, and old.

MELANIE (*quickly*) : No.

PAUL : Middle-aged then.

MELANIE : Yes.

PAUL : Educated, cultured, and useless.

MELANIE : Yes.

II

PAUL : And equally penniless.

MELANIE : Yes.

PAUL : But fortunately possessed of an inherent talent for obtaining credit.

MELANIE : Fortunately.

PAUL : You are my only possible business asset.

MELANIE : Let us talk of something else.

PAUL (*continuing*) : Attractive, young, and, surprisingly enough, a virgin.

MELANIE : Please stop now. I will be good, really I will.

PAUL : You are my ward, are you not ? The forsaken daughter of my dear old friend the Marquis de Tramont ?

MELANIE : Yes, Paul.

PAUL : You spent your lisping carefree childhood in an old grey château, didn't you ?

MELANIE : What's "lisping" ?

PAUL : Never mind. (*He stalks round the room, engrossed in the story.*) You have never been to Paris in your life, have you ?

MELANIE : No, Paul.

PAUL : What is Le Petit Girondin ?

MELANIE : I suppose it must be a very little man from Bordeaux.

PAUL : Correct. (*He goes to the table, places a chair for her to sit.*) Come ! Business ! Now then, what did Lord Sheere say to you last night ?

MELANIE (*seated*) : Not very much, but he was very ardent.

PAUL : Good. He is coming here this morning.

MELANIE : This morning ?

PAUL : Yes. I wrote him a little note from you.

12

I will receive him and when I have talked to him for a little he will propose marriage.

MELANIE : He seemed last night to wish for something a little less binding.

PAUL : Never mind. When he proposes, you will accept him.

MELANIE : When may I love somebody please ?

PAUL : Not until you are safely married, and then only with the greatest discretion.

MELANIE (*quietly*) : I see.

PAUL (*after a slight pause*) : What's the matter ?

MELANIE : It doesn't feel like my birthday any more. (*Singing.*)

> A cloud has passed across the sun,
> The morning seems no longer gay.

PAUL (*speaking*) : I want to get on with these bills. You had better go and dress.

MELANIE (*listlessly*) : Very well—— (*Singing.*)

> With so much business to be done,
> Even the sea looks grey.

PAUL (*speaking*) : Don't be silly.

MELANIE (*singing.*)

> C'est vrai. C'est vrai.
> It seems that all the joy has faded from the day
> As though the foolish world no longer wants
>   to play.

PAUL (*speaking.*) : Go and dress.

MELANIE (*speaking*) : What shall I wear ? A black crêpe with a little bonnet ?

PAUL : What on earth is the matter with you this morning ?

MELANIE : White, white for a bride. But the sun ought to shine on a bride.

PAUL : You're not a bride yet.

MELANIE : But I shall be soon, shall I not ?   A very quiet aristocratic bride with a discreet heart ! (*Singing.*)

> You ask me to have a discreet heart
> Until marriage is out of the way,
> But what if I meet
> With a sweetheart so sweet
> That my wayward heart cannot obey
> A single word that you may say ?

PAUL (*speaking*) : Then we shall have to go away.

MELANIE (*singing*) :

> No.
> For there is nowhere we could go
> Where we could hide from what we know
> Is true.

PAUL (*speaking*) : Do stop talking nonsense.

MELANIE (*speaking*) : It is not nonsense. You are so sure that everything in life can be arranged just so, like arithmetic.

PAUL : Why not ?   Emotion is so very untidy.

MELANIE : The sun has come out again.   I feel a little better.

PAUL (*writing something on one of the bills*) : Good.

MELANIE (*goes to the window humming, then returns to the desk and leaning across it she pats* PAUL'S *hand*) : I'm sorry.   (*Singing.*)

> Don't be afraid I'll betray you
> And destroy all the plans you have made,
> But even your schemes
> Must leave room for my dreams.
> So when all I owe to you is paid
> I'll still have something of my own,
> A little prize that's mine alone.

> I'll follow my secret heart
> My whole life through,
> I'll keep all my dreams apart
> Till one comes true.
> No matter what price is paid,
> What stars may fade
> Above,
> I'll follow my secret heart
> Till I find love.

When she has sung this waltz refrain she goes into her room. PAUL *rings a little bell on the desk.* ROSE *enters.*

PAUL : Rose, prenez le plateau——

ROSE *takes up the tray.*

PAUL : I am expecting the Marquis of Sheere. He should be here at any moment.

ROSE (*raising her eyebrows*) : Oh!

PAUL : Why do you say " Oh " like that?

ROSE : It seems funny a gentleman of his position calling in the morning.

PAUL : Why funny?

ROSE : In my last place the gentlemen always called in the evening.

PAUL : I think the sooner you wipe your last place from your mind the better.

ROSE : Yes, sir.

There is a rat-tat-tat on the door downstairs, and ROSE, *with a knowing look in her eye, goes out.* PAUL *rises as* ROSE *re-enters.*

ROSE (*announcing*) : The Marquis of Sheere.

The MARQUIS OF SHEERE (EDWARD) *comes in quickly, wearing an air of expectancy, which changes to slight confusion when he sees* PAUL. *He is a good-looking romantic young man in the twenties.*

PAUL (*going to him*): Lord Sheere?

EDWARD: Yes.

ROSE *goes out.*

PAUL: Allow me to introduce myself. I am the Duc de Chaucigny-Varennes.

EDWARD: Oh, how do you do?

They shake hands.

PAUL: Melanie, my ward, will be here in a moment.

EDWARD (*relieved, but puzzled*): Oh, I'm so glad.

PAUL: In the meantime, can I offer you a little wine?

EDWARD: No, thank you.

PAUL: At least I beg you will be seated. (*He indicates the sofa and draws up a chair for himself.*)

EDWARD (*sitting down*): Thank you.

PAUL: Tell me, do you speak French?

EDWARD: Oui, un peu.

PAUL: I never think that's enough, do you?

EDWARD (*slightly crestfallen*): I suppose not.

PAUL (*charmingly*): Never mind, we will talk English. In the old days before the revolution my mother engaged an English governess for all of us. I remember she had a very pink nose, but her syntax was above reproach.

EDWARD: I'm so glad.

PAUL: It is not a matter for unrestrained jubilation, but we will leave it for the moment as we have things of more importance to discuss.

EDWARD: Have we?

PAUL: I understand that you wish to marry my ward?

EDWARD (*rising, extremely startled*): What! I beg your pardon?

16

PAUL : You seem embarrassed ?

EDWARD (*floundering*) : Well—I—er—I——

PAUL (*sententiously*) : Ah, Love, Love, that fond foolish ecstasy ! It ties the tongue in knots as well as the heart, does it not ?

EDWARD : Yes, but you see—I really feel——

PAUL : Come now, there is no need to look so confused. I am a man of the world, old enough to be your father—you can be perfectly frank with me. Please sit down again.

    EDWARD *sits*.

EDWARD : I had no idea that Melanie, Mademoiselle de Tramont, had a—a——

PAUL : Guardian.

EDWARD (*gulping*) : Guardian.

PAUL : She is the daughter of my dear old friend the Marquis de Tramont. The whole family was wiped out, father, mother, five sons and four daughters.

EDWARD : A large family.

PAUL : Very large. Melanie alone escaped. She was smuggled out of the château by one of the serving maids, a rude homely girl, who, after many vicissitudes, managed to convey her to me in Amiens, where I was in hiding.

EDWARD : How old was she ?

PAUL : A mere child.

EDWARD : I see.

PAUL (*leaning forward*) : I have watched over her and cared for her all these years. I have seen her grow from childhood to girlhood, from girlhood to womanhood. We have wandered together lonely exiles, through strange countries. Her youth and sweetness have kept my heart alive when everything I loved was dead, and now you come, a stranger, and wish to take her from me——

EDWARD : You misunderstand, sir, I assure you——

PAUL (*holding up his hand*) : No, no, do not protest. I understand only too well. I have known that this would happen. It is the penalty of age to be lonely, and I am quite prepared.

EDWARD (*firmly*) : I have not proposed marriage to Melanie.

PAUL : That does credit both to your upbringing and your personal integrity. I unfortunately am not in a position to put your fears entirely at rest. I cannot tell for certain whether or not she really loves you, but, if you will take the advice of an old man, don't give up hope, don't despair too soon—— (*He rings the bell on the desk.*)

> ROSE *enters very quickly, having obviously been listening at the door.*

ROSE : You rang, sir ?

PAUL : Ask Mademoiselle if she would be kind enough to come here.

ROSE : Yes, sir.

> *She goes into the bedroom.*

PAUL : You understand, her happiness is all that matters to me. I have naturally taken care to make discreet enquiries as to your character and way of life, forgive me being frank, but as a foreigner, such precautions I think may be excused. You may rest assured that at the earliest possible moment, I shall give myself the honour of calling upon your parents.

EDWARD (*terrified*) : For God's sake don't do that !

PAUL (*smiling fondly*) : Foolish boy !

MELANIE *comes in from the bedroom, very beautifully dressed, and rather pale. She curtseys to* PAUL.

MELANIE : Bonjour, mon oncle.

PAUL (*sweetly*) : Fie donc, Melanie. Anglais, je t'en prie. N'oublie pas ta promesse.

MELANIE : Non. I am sorry. (*She curtseys to* EDWARD.) Good morning, Monsieur le Marquis.

EDWARD : Good morning, Mademoiselle !

PAUL : There is no need to be so formal, my dear. We all understand one another. Lord Sheere and I have had a little talk.

MELANIE (*slightly apprehensive*) : Oh—vraiment ?

PAUL (*taking both her hands*) : My *little* Melanie.

MELANIE (*drawing back—suspiciously*) : Qu'est-ce qu'il y a ?

PAUL : Qu'est-ce qu'il y a ? (*In a very beautiful voice.*) Be gentle with him, my Melanie, gentle and kind. True love is over sensitive. I will leave you for a while.

MELANIE : No, Paul—please stay——

PAUL : It is better that I should go. (*He places his hand upon* EDWARD'S *shoulder and gazes searchingly into his eyes for a moment.*) My boy !

PAUL *bows gracefully and goes out, leaving behind him an atmosphere of considerable embarrassment.* MELANIE *and* EDWARD *stand staring at each other until she can bear it no longer, and breaks the strain by going to the window.*

MELANIE (*at window*) : It is a very nice day, is it not ?

EDWARD : Very nice.

MELANIE : So pretty—everything here in England looks so fresh and clean—regardez ce petit bateau à voiles—sail boat ?

EDWARD (*coming also to the window*): Yes—that's a sailing boat.

MELANIE: Léger sous le soleil, comme un papillon blanc——

EDWARD: Yes. Oh, yes, indeed——

    A pipe organ begins to play softly in the street below.

MELANIE: Music too.

EDWARD (*staring at her*): Yes—music too——

MELANIE: Why do you look like that?

EDWARD: It's true.

MELANIE: What is true? Je ne comprends pas——

EDWARD: What he said—your guardian—about love.

MELANIE (*turning away*): Oh.

EDWARD: I didn't understand.

MELANIE: The music is too loud.

EDWARD: Why not? Why shouldn't it be loud? It plays everywhere, doesn't it—that sort of music—all over the world?

MELANIE: You speak so quickly—please do not speak so quickly.

EDWARD: Who are you, really?

MELANIE (*she sits on the sofa, closing her eyes as though repeating a lesson*): I am Melanie de Tramont, the daughter of the Marquis de Tramont, he—my father—was killed in the revolution—my mother also, and my little brother Armand——

EDWARD: And your other brothers and sisters?

MELANIE: All dead.

EDWARD: What were their names?

MELANIE: Je ne comprends pas.

EDWARD: How many were there?

MELANIE: Many—a great many.

20

EDWARD : You loved them ?

MELANIE : Yes, they were very nice.

EDWARD : And your mother and father ?

MELANIE : Very nice indeed.

EDWARD : Guillotined ?

MELANIE : Please—I cannot bear to speak of it.

EDWARD : I'm sorry.

MELANIE : It is long ago now, but I can never quite forget.

EDWARD : And your guardian—you love him ?

MELANIE : Yes.

EDWARD : I see.

MELANIE : As a father.

EDWARD : Who are you—really ?

MELANIE : Oh—go away—please go away.

EDWARD : Who are you—really ?

MELANIE : I do not know.

EDWARD (*suddenly he sits next to her*) : I love you.

MELANIE (*painfully*) : No.

EDWARD : Before, when I have seen you in the distance, and last night when I talked to you, I wanted you—but now—now I love you——

MELANIE : No, no——

EDWARD : It's true, I know it—it happened suddenly a moment ago—it feels strange, as though I were not quite awake, and yet at the same time more awake than I have ever been before. You see I am not very old, not very experienced yet, and it's—it's the first time.

MELANIE (*she rises, walks away, clasping and unclasping her hands*) : Oh—this is very uneasy.

EDWARD : Why ? Didn't you expect it ?

MELANIE : No—not like this.

21   C

EDWARD : You know—you wanted me to love you, didn't you ? Both you and your—your guardian— wanted me to love you——

MELANIE (*retreating from him*) : No, no——

EDWARD : You see I am not quite so young as all that, not quite a fool—my eyes are wide open—there is a lot that I don't understand, a trick, some sort of trick, I feel it with all my instincts, but I don't care—I feel more than that—I feel that you are very lovely, and very sweet too, and that is enough—will you please—please be my wife ?

MELANIE (*sinking into a chair and covering her face with her hands*) : Laissez-moi, je vous en supplie, laissez-moi——

EDWARD : Look at me.

MELANIE : Non, non——

EDWARD (*gently taking her hands away from her face*) : Melanie.

MELANIE (*whispering*) : Go away—please, please go away.

EDWARD : Very well. (*He smiles rather tremulously.*) But I shall come back.

MELANIE : Yes, come back—but think a little before you come back—see me once again from the distance——

EDWARD : I am afraid it is too late for that.

MELANIE (*curtseying, with her eyes averted from him*) : Thank you, Monsieur le Marquis.

EDWARD (*bowing*) : Mademoiselle !

> He looks at her for a moment, and then goes out swiftly. When he has gone she goes to the window and sings very softly, " I'll follow my secret heart " as the lights fade on the scene.

ACT I

Scene IV

Quartette : " Regency Rakes."

Verse

You may think
Looking at the four of us
Food and drink
Constitute the core of us.
That may be,
But still you'll see
Our names on posterity's page.
You will read
Histories galore of us
Strutting England's stage.
We represent
To a certain extent
The ineffable scent
Of our Age.

Refrain

We're Regency Rakes
And each of us takes
A personal pride
In the thickness of hide
Which prevents us from seeing
How vulgar we're being
Without making us wince.

23

We're ruthless and rude
And boast of a crude
And lordly disdain
Both for mind and for brain.
Tho' obtuse and slow-witted,
We're not to be pitied,
For we follow the Prince,
Every orgy
With our Georgie
Lasts till dawn without a lull.
We can venture
Without censure
To be noisy, drunk, and dull !
We revel in Sport,
Madeira, and Port,
And when we pass out
With Sclerosis and Gout,
All our children will rue our mistakes,
Roystering Regency Rakes.

2nd Refrain
We're Regency Rakes
And each of us makes
A personal issue
Of adipose tissue
But still notwithstanding,
Our stomachs expanding,
We all yearn for romance.
We frequently start
Affairs of the heart,
Sublimely unheeding
That long over-feeding
Has made so disgusting

Our loving or lusting
That girls eye us askance,
Tho' we wonder
As we blunder
Into this or that bordel,
Whom we know there,
Why we go there,
But we're far too drunk to tell,
Tho' over-jocose,
Unfunny and gross,
We don't lose a fraction
Of self-satisfaction.
Complacency never forsakes
Roystering Regency Rakes !

ACT I

SCENE V

The Scene is MELANIE'S *room again. It is about three
o'clock in the afternoon.*

When the Curtain rises the room is empty. Presently
ROSE *ushers in* SOPHIE OTFORD, MARTHA JAMES
and MRS. DRAGON. MRS. DRAGON *is an ample
lady attired austerely in black, enlivened here and there
by an occasional glitter of jet.*

ROSE : Mademoiselle will be with you in a moment.

SOPHIE : Thank you.

ROSE : I will inform Mademoiselle that you are
here.

MARTHA : Thank you.

SOPHIE (*conversationally*) : Such a nice little house.
Which is the Duc de Varennes' room ?

ROSE : Monsieur le Dook don't live here.

MARTHA (*triumphantly*) : There you are.

> *She goes up to examine the quality of the wine glasses
> on the sideboard.*

SOPHIE : He just visits Mademoiselle, I suppose ?

ROSE : Yes, every morning.

MARTHA : Only in the morning ?

> *She tests one of the glasses with a snap of her finger—
> it rings clearly.*

SOPHIE : Don't be crude, Martha.

ROSE : Monsieur le Dook is Mademoiselle's guardian.

SOPHIE : That's right, my dear.   You're a very good girl.

MARTHA : Have you been with Mademoiselle long ?

ROSE : Ever since she arrived in England, Madame.

MARTHA : I seem to know your face.   Have I ever seen you before ?

ROSE : I don't think you could have, Madame.

SOPHIE : Where do you come from ?

ROSE : I was brought up in Wales, Madame. In a little village by the sea.

MARTHA : You haven't got a Welsh accent.

ROSE : I know. That's what's so funny.   My mother and father never 'ave been able to understand it.

SOPHIE : Well, if they can't, nobody can.

MARTHA : Were you engaged by Monsieur le Duc, or by Mademoiselle herself ?

SOPHIE : Martha !

MARTHA : Well, I want to know.

ROSE : I was engaged through a friend.

SOPHIE : Who ?

ROSE (*exasperated*) : Mrs. Edwards, the one who arranged your little affair with Lord Meadowfield.

SOPHIE : Don't be impudent.

ROSE : Well, mind your own business, then.
    She goes out.

MARTHA : I thought as much.   Do sit down, Dragon.
    MRS. DRAGON *sits down.*

SOPHIE : Guardian, indeed !

MARTHA : None of my gentlemen have ever spoken to her alone yet.

SOPHIE : Not even His Grace ?

MARTHA : Not even His Grace.

27

Rose *returns from the bedroom and the visitors invent charming conversation, until* Rose *goes out the other door*.

Sophie : There's something fishy about it.

Martha : There's always something fishy about the French!

Melanie *enters.   Everyone curtseys with great enthusiasm.*

Melanie : Ah, chères Mesdames, mes chères Mesdames, comme je suis enchantée de vous voir—

Sophie : This is Mrs. Dragon.

Melanie : 'Ow do you do!

Mrs. Dragon *curtseys, but doesn't say anything.*

Martha : We've been admiring your charming house.

Melanie : I am so glad, please sit you down, and the tea will be here soon.

The guests sit on the sofa.

Sophie (*with an effort*) : Est-ce que vous trouvez que Brighton est joli?

Melanie (*smiling gaily*) : Ah ça, c'est défendu. Monsieur le Duc ne me permet pas de parler un mot de français, parce que, enfin, c'est absolument nécessaire que je fasse des progrès en anglais.

Sophie : Oh—er oui—je vois, je vois.

They all laugh.

Melanie : Mais je souffre, ah, mon Dieu, comme je souffre! Quand je tâche de chercher les phrases, je me sens perdu. C'est idiot!

Sophie (*giving up*) : There now.

Melanie : Mais vous savez je fais des progrès, mais quand même je continue à dire des bêtises affreuses, surtout lorsque je me trouve dans une situation délicate. C'est vraiment inouï. Ma langue fourche, et je dis des choses que je ne devrais pas, et Paul, Monsieur le Duc, me regarde d'un petit air narquois, et je veux cacher ma tête comme une autruche.

SOPHIE : I always love the Austrians.

MARTHA : Such charming manners.

     ROSE *enters with the tea-things which she sets up on a little table.*

MELANIE : Please take the tea?

SOPHIE : Thank you.

     They all sit round the table.

MELANIE (*dispensing tea*) : It was so kind of you to arrive.

SOPHIE : Martha and I are giving a little party this evening, just cards and conversation and a few friends. His Grace the Duke of Twickenham has promised to honour us, we would be so pleased if you would come too.

MELANIE : It would delight me, but I fear I cannot.

MARTHA : What a shame! You have another engagement?

MELANIE : No, I have to work in the evening with Monsieur le Duc.

SOPHIE : As well as the morning? How tiring!

MELANIE : Another time I should be so glad if you will invite me.

MARTHA : But, of course, we would like to know you better. When we spoke to you the other day on the Steyne we thought you looked so nice and so lonely, with only your maid for company.

SOPHIE : That was a delightful bonnet you were wearing.

MELANIE : The green plush?

SOPHIE : Yes.

MELANIE : I have two new ones, more pretty, and a

cramoisie dress, velvet, for walking—you would like to see?

MARTHA : Oh yes.

MELANIE : They all came from the little shop of Mrs. Baxter—Rose, please bring the boxes from my room.

ROSE : Yes, Mademoiselle.

She curtseys and goes out.

SOPHIE : Mrs. Baxter is very expensive.

MELANIE : Alas yes, but the line she makes is good.

MARTHA : Are you staying here long?

MELANIE : I do not really know. My guardian has the business to make, when that is done we will return.

SOPHIE : What is his business?

MARTHA *and* DRAGON *are "all ears."*

MELANIE : It is financial—I do not know words to explain correctly, but there must be a—a—transaction. That I know very well.

SOPHIE : I see.

MARTHA : Were you born in Paris?

MELANIE : Oh, no, I lived as a child on the Loire— an old grey château, with a small water where there were swans—

SOPHIE : Very pretty.

MELANIE : Yes, it was pretty; I spent all my early days lisping there.

MARTHA : You haven't got a lisp now.

MELANIE : No, I lost it in the Revolution.

ROSE *enters from bedroom carrying several dress and hat boxes.*

ROSE (*putting them down*): There, Mademoiselle.

MELANIE : Merci, Rose. (*To* SOPHIE). You wish to see? (*To* ROSE.) The mull dress with marabout and the turban——

30

Rose *opens one of the boxes and takes out a turban.*
Sophie *and* Martha *give appropriate cries of appreciation.* Rose *opens another box and takes out a dress. The music, which has been playing softly throughout the scene, falls into a more set rhythm, and* Rose, Martha, Sophie *and* Melanie *sing a quartette while they all try on different garments and hats. In course of this, a fife-and-drum band is heard outside on the Parade, and they all run to the window to wave to the soldiers marching by. Towards the end of the song, there is a rat-tat-tat at the front door. None of them hear except* Rose, *who runs down to answer it.*

Quartette:

Sophie :	Charming! Charming! Charming!
Rose :	This gown is for the morning,
	When Mademoiselle goes out,
	As Madame sees
	In the slightest breeze
	The feathers float about.
Sophie : Martha: }	Charming! Charming! Charming!
Rose	This jacket is for driving,
	Or strolling beside the sea.
Sophie :	Pretty as it seems to be
	It's a little too full in the sleeves for me.
All :	Ah la la la—la la—la la.
Sophie :	Pretty as it seems to be
	It's a trifle full in the sleeves for me.
Melanie :	This dress is for the evening,
	To wear when I meet my dear,
	Whenever that may chance to be.
	In the moment that he looks at me

31

The skies will suddenly clear.
I'll know him then for my destiny,
And so through each changing year
I shall leave him never, for evermore.

ROSE : Don't you think these pinks and blues
are sweet.
This stuff is sent especially from France.

MELANIE : Oh, please, please say you think these
satin shoes are sweet
They make me feel I want to dance.

Danser—Danser—La Vie est gaie,
Je me sens libre, abandonnée.
Le chant trouble mon cœur
Qui donc m'envoie ce doux bonheur,
Mon corps, mes pieds, ensorcelés
Légers, ailes, vont s'envoler.
Tra la la la la—la la la—la la la la la,
Tra la la la la—la la la—lalalalala la—la—la

SOPHIE :
MARTHA :
ROSE :   } Look for a love that's gay and sweet.
MELANIE :

SOPHIE :
MARTHA :
ROSE :   } Music to guide your dancing feet.
MELANIE :

SOPHIE :   Follow your secret strain
              And you won't be living in vain,
MARTHA :   Treat your desire by word and deed
              Lightly—lightly—
ROSE :   And if at first you don't succeed
              Try and try again.

MELANIE :   Mon corps, mes pieds, ensorcelés
                Légers, ailes, vont s'envoler.
                Tra la la la la—la la la—la la la—la—la
                Tra la la la la—la la la——

SOPHIE (*speaking*) : Soldiers!

MARTHA (*rushing to window*) : Quickly—let's see——

ROSE (*also rushing to window*) : I do love soldiers.

MELANIE (*joining them*) : Oh, they are so pretty, so pretty in their red coats.

SOPHIE : They're some of the guards from the Pavilion.

ROSE (*singing*) :   When I see the soldiers marching by
                With fife and drum
                Beneath a summer sky

SOPHIE : ⎫
  and   ⎬ Little dears who love to do and die
MARTHA : ⎭

ROSE :   My spirit sings
           And spreads its wings to fly.

SOPHIE (*spoken*) : Nicely put, my girl, but a trifle affected.

ROSE : Well, it's true.

MARTHA : Look at the officer leading them.

SOPHIE : I must admit he could leave his shoes under my bed any time he liked.

ROSE (*singing*) :
           Think of all the battles they have won

MELANIE (*singing*) :
           So brave and strong
           They march along
           Like little boys
           Who play with toys
           For fun.

SOPHIE and MARTHA :	Little boys who frolic in the sun.
ROSE :	Right—right—right left right——
ALL :	Right—right—right left right left——

March, little soldiers, we all adore
    you,
We'd swoon before you
If we thought that you would care,
Whate'er befalls you,
Where duty calls you,
We should love to be there,
To share
All your troubles, but we'd never dare,
But we're quite prepared to cheer you to
    victory,
To joy or despair,
Joy or despair,
That's only fair.
Dear little soldiers,
Should you admire us
And feel desirous
On returning from the fray,
We'd soon surrender,
You'd find us tender
And sublimely unresisting
In assisting
You to spend
Your soldiers' pay pay pay.

At the end of the song, when MELANIE, MARTHA
and SOPHIE *are twirling gaily about the room,* ROSE
re-enters and announces in rather gloomy tones: The Duke

*and Duchess of Beneden. The music stops dead as they
enter. They are elderly, haughty, and grim.*

DUCHESS (*stiffly*) : Mademoiselle de Tramont?

MELANIE (*curtseying*) : Oui!

DUCHESS : I am the Duchess of Beneden. Please
forgive us for calling upon you so—so unexpectedly. I
believe you are acquainted with my son, Lord Sheere?

DUKE : A moment, my love, just a moment, do not
rush matters.

MELANIE : I think you do not know Mrs. James and
Mrs. Otford.

DUCHESS (*icily*) : I do not.

MELANIE (*charmingly*) : Then it is easy that you should
because they are here.

    *She indicates them with a polite gesture; they both
    curtsey low. The* DUCHESS *bows almost imperceptibly.*

SOPHIE : This is Mrs. Dragon.

MARTHA : Of Dorset.

DUCHESS (*without the faintest sign of recognition*) :
Indeed?

SOPHIE (*after a slight pause*) : Nice weather, taken all
in all?

MELANIE : Will you not sit yourselves down?

DUCHESS : No, thank you.

MELANIE : Perhaps you would like the tea.

DUCHESS (*with an atrocious accent*) : Non merci. Je
pense qu'il serait mieux si nous parlons en français.

MELANIE : Au contraire, Madame, my friends do not
understand French.

MARTHA (*with great refinement*) : Oh, please don't
bother about us, we shall have to go now, anyhow.

MELANIE : Oh, no, please stay a little longer.

SOPHIE : We really must go, we have an appointment

35

with the Duke of Twickenham. (*Pertly to the* DUCHESS.) He is your cousin, I believe.

> *The* DUCHESS *turns away without answering.*

MARTHA : Come on, Dragon. (*She goes to the door.*)

SOPHIE : Good-bye, my dear Duke—it's ages since we last met, isn't it? Do you remember? That New Year's party at Mrs. Johnstone's—a very gay evening, wasn't it? (*She turns to* MELANIE.) Au revoir, Mademoiselle. (*She curtseys.*)

MARTHA (*also curtseying*) : We must meet again very soon.

SOPHIE : Et merci beaucoup!

MELANIE : Au revoir.

> MRS. DRAGON *does a slightly abortive curtsey to everyone and the three of them go out, followed reluctantly by* ROSE. *When the door has closed behind them the* DUCHESS *turns.*

DUCHESS : As I said before, I believe you are acquainted with my son.

MELANIE : Yes.

DUCHESS : You would be doing my husband and myself a great service if you discontinued that acquaintance.

MELANIE : You are come here to ask a service?

DUKE : Yes, Mademoiselle, we have.

MELANIE (*to the* DUCHESS) : Then I do not understand how your manner is so unpolite.

DUKE : My wife is upset, naturally upset.

MELANIE : Pourquoi?

DUKE : Edward is our only son.

MELANIE : Is that not more your fault than mine?

DUCHESS : It is no use bandying words, Frederick, and wasting time. (*To* MELANIE.) I am a woman of the world, Mademoiselle, and I fully realise your position.

The DUKE *looks appraisingly at* MELANIE, *through his quizzing glass.*

MELANIE : I fear I do not understand.

DUCHESS : Things may be different in France, I am sure I do not know about that since that dreadful Bonaparte has ruined the country, but here in England, there are still two distinct worlds. You belong to one, and my son belongs to the other. Those two worlds do not mix.

MELANIE : I would prefer that you speak to my guardian of these things.

DUCHESS (*sniffing*) : Guardian.

MELANIE : Monsieur le Duc de Chaucigny-Varennes.

DUKE : Perhaps, my love, that after all would be a better plan.

DUCHESS : Please, Frederick, allow me to deal with this. (*To* MELANIE.) My son is infatuated with you, but he is young and that infatuation will not last. It must not last. I wish you to give me your word that you will never see him again. My husband and I are fully prepared to compensate you within reason.

MELANIE : Compensate?   Que-ce que c'est ça— compensate?

DUCHESS (*laconically*) : Money.

MELANIE : Money! You will pay me money?

DUCHESS : Yes.

MELANIE : To see your son never again?

DUCHESS : Yes.

MELANIE : If I love him, what then?

DUCHESS : That is beside the point.

MELANIE : I think you will perhaps go away now.

DUCHESS : Five hundred pounds.

MELANIE : He is very charming, your son, and his eyes are very clear and true. I think he will be angry.

DUCHESS : A thousand pounds.

MELANIE (*ringing the bell on the desk*) : I am tired, Madame. I cannot sit down until you go.

DUKE: Mademoiselle, I beg of you—my wife is distrait——

MELANIE: That is not of interest to me.

DUCHESS (*losing control slightly*) : I would like to make one thing clear to you. My son is not yet of age. If he marries without his parents' consent he will not have a penny. Not a penny! Do you understand that?

DUKE : Georgina, Georgina—please——

MELANIE : He would make a very sweet husband, your son, even without a penny, because he is kind.

ROSE *enters, and stands by the door.*

DUKE : Come, Georgina.

The DUCHESS *looks at* MELANIE *furiously for a moment in silence, and then, without a word, turns her back on her and sweeps out of the room followed by the* DUKE. *The* DUKE *turns at the door and bows with the suspicion of a smile.* ROSE *follows them out, and* MELANIE *runs to the window to peep through the curtains at them. In a moment or two* ROSE *returns.*

MELANIE : Ça y est!

ROSE : What's that?

MELANIE : Some Madeira, quickly, my legs will not stand. (*She sinks down on the sofa.*)

ROSE *runs to a little side table and pours her out a glass of Madeira.*

ROSE : My goodness! Her face when she went out!

MELANIE : Mon Dieu! Her face when she came in.

ROSE : That bonnet!

MELANIE (*starting to laugh*) : Like a pheasant.

ROSE : Feathers and all. (*She starts to laugh too.*)

MELANIE (*laughing more wildly*): The Duke—the poor, poor man——

ROSE : Looked like a corpse, and no wonder——

They are both laughing weakly when PAUL *comes into the room.*

PAUL : Why was the front door open?

ROSE : Oh, dear!

PAUL : What is the matter?

MELANIE (*hysterically*) : Five hundred pounds—a thousand pounds—not enough—not quite enough—but better than nothing!

PAUL : That will do, Rose.

ROSE : Yes, sir.

She goes out, wiping her eyes.

PAUL : Now, what has happened?

MELANIE : Je vous raconterai ce qui vient de passer. On m'a insulté et si cela ne me faisait pas tant rire j'aurais envie de pleurer.

PAUL : Qui vous a insulté? Que voulez-vous dire?

MELANIE : La très charmante mère de Monsieur le Marquis, ils sortent d'ici, le Duc et la Duchesse, je ne suis pas encore assez bien élevée—j'avais envie de lui cracher à la figure—c'est un grossier vieux chameau—elle s'est conduite avec moi comme envers une gruel

PAUL : J'espère que vous ne lui avez pas donné de raison pour vous prendre comme telle.

MELANIE : Du reste tout ceci est de votre faute. Je n'avais aucune envie de connaître tous ces gens. J'étais bien plus heureuse là où j'étais.

PAUL : Ça c'est idiot!

MELANIE : Mais c'est vrai! Vous voulez que je

39

l'épouse votre Marquis? Eh bien, soit: et puis après, vous verrez, il sera sans le sou, et moi, je serai forcée de retourner chanter dans un café—Madame la Marquise au café chantant! Ça sera du joli, et ça sera bien faire pour vous!

> *There is a rat-tat-tat at the door.* MELANIE *runs to the window.*

C'est lui, le Duc, et tout seul cette fois.

PAUL : I'll talk to him.

MELANIE : No.

PAUL : But, my dear Melanie——

MELANIE : Go into the bedroom.

PAUL : But I——

MELANIE : Go quickly—listen at the door—and do not come out until I say——

PAUL : You will call me?

MELANIE : I will say, "The sea is so pretty." Go on—quickly——

> PAUL *goes into the bedroom.* MELANIE *pushes the boxes to the back of the room.* ROSE *enters.*

ROSE (*with a slight leer*) : The Duke of Beneden.

> MELANIE *is now seated, posing for the interview. The* DUKE *enters. He bows with almost overdone politeness.* ROSE *goes out.*

DUKE : Mademoiselle, I—I—have returned.

MELANIE : I see you have.

DUKE : I ask your forgiveness.

MELANIE : Thank you.

DUKE : My wife——

MELANIE : She is upset?

DUKE : Yes.

MELANIE : Distrait?

DUKE : Exactly.

MELANIE : Ill-mannered?

DUKE : Yes—er—I mean—well, you understand?

MELANIE : I do not understand.

DUKE (*with a charming smile*) : Please try.

MELANIE : That is better.

DUKE : You are very pretty, Mademoiselle, and very charming.

MELANIE : Oh!

DUKE : I am sure that you cannot possibly be hard-hearted.

MELANIE : It is difficult to have the soft heart when one is insulted.

DUKE : My wife does not understand, as I understand.

MELANIE (*averting her eyes*) : Oh, Monsieur le Duc.

DUKE : Do you love my son?

MELANIE (*still looking down*) : I do not know.

DUKE : He loves you?

MELANIE : Yes.

DUKE : Do you wish to marry him?

MELANIE : Please—I do not know.

DUKE : All his money is controlled by his mother; if you did become his wife, she would cut him off entirely.

MELANIE : I see.

DUKE : Whereas I——

MELANIE (*looking up sharply*) : You?

DUKE (*with slight embarrassment*) : I find myself in an extremely awkward position.

MELANIE : Why?

DUKE : I do not want to bore you with my troubles, but you are so sympathetic.

MELANIE (*going to him*) : What is it you would say?

41

DUKE : I have a little house in London, a dear little house very nicely furnished just near Berkeley Square, and it is unhappy because it is not lived in, the pretty furniture is covered up and the blinds are drawn.

MELANIE : How sad!

DUKE : You see I am an old man now.

MELANIE : Non, Monsieur.

DUKE : Well, elderly.

MELANIE : Perhaps.

DUKE : And my heart, like the house, is covered up, and the blinds are drawn.

MELANIE (*turning away*) : Your wife, does she know about the little house?

DUKE : No.

MELANIE : And your heart? Does she know about that?

DUKE : No.

MELANIE (*resting her hand lightly on his arm*) : Poor Monsieur le Duc, life is very difficult, is it not?

DUKE : I knew you would understand. (*He holds her hand, almost as though he didn't notice it.*)

MELANIE : What is the rent of the little house?

DUKE : That is all paid.

MELANIE : And is there a little carriage with white horses and a footman on the box?

DUKE : How did you guess?

MELANIE : And every month, the bills of the house? They will be much?

DUKE (*tentatively*) : Two hundred pounds?

MELANIE (*firmly*) : Three hundred pounds.

DUKE (*smiling*) : Three hundred pounds.

MELANIE : On the first day of every month?

DUKE (*pulling her a little towards him*) : On the first

42

day of every month.

MELANIE (*surrendering*) : But I do not yet know about London.

DUKE : It is delightful! You would love it.

MELANIE : But I love it here in Brighton.

He takes her in his arms.

The sea is so pretty.

PAUL *enters from the bedroom. The* DUKE *starts back and hurriedly disentangles himself from* MELANIE.

PAUL (*sternly*) : Melanie!

MELANIE (*terrified*) : Ah, mon Dieu!

PAUL : Monsieur, I do not think I have the pleasure of your acquaintance.

DUKE : I am the Duke of Beneden.

PAUL : Melanie, go to your room.

MELANIE : Mais, mon oncle, je——

PAUL : Immediately. Do as I tell you.

MELANIE : Oui, mon oncle.

She drops a hurried little curtsey to the DUKE, *curtseys to* PAUL, *makes a wry face and goes out.*

PAUL : Now then, Monsieur!

DUKE : I see it all now.

PAUL : You are the father of the Marquis of Sheere?

DUKE : Yes.

PAUL : I see. Good-bye, Monsieur.

DUKE : I would like to explain.

PAUL : There is nothing to explain. It is all de-pressingly clear. (*He rings the bell.*) I will call upon you and the Duchess later when I have decided what course to take.

DUKE : Look here, sir, I——

PAUL : The Duc de Chaucigny-Varennes. At your service.

43

ROSE *enters.*

Rose, kindly conduct his Grace downstairs.

ROSE : Yes, sir.

DUKE : I fear you don't quite understand. There is some mistake——

PAUL : There is a very grave mistake, and I understand perfectly. Good-bye. (*He bows abruptly.*)

> The DUKE *still hesitates for a moment, then bows stiffly and goes out followed by* ROSE, *who has the impertinence to wink broadly at* PAUL *over her shoulder.*
>
> The *music swells and* MELANIE *puts her head round the bedroom door.* PAUL *beckons to her, and they both tiptoe in time to the music to the window, where, shaking with silent laughter, they peep through the curtains as the lights fade.*

ACT I

SCENE VI

TRIO : MARTHA, SOPHIE *and* DRAGON.
"THERE'S ALWAYS SOMETHING FISHY ABOUT THE
FRENCH."

Verse 1

SOPHIE :   A life of Love is curious
      But not injurious
      If you are wise,

MARTHA : For you get pleasure,
      Leisure,
      Knowledge to treasure
      After the gay life dies;

SOPHIE :   Tho' men we seldom bind to us
      They're often kind to us,

MARTHA : And entre nous

BOTH :   English Gentlemen,
      Spanish Noblemen,
      Indian Merchantmen too
      Always play the game,
      Never cause us shame.

Refrain 1

BOTH :   But there's always something fishy about
      the French!
      Whether Prince or Politician
      We've a sinister suspicion

45

That behind their "savoir faire"
They share
A common contempt
For every mother's son of us.
Tho' they smile and smirk
We know they're out for dirty work,
So we're most polite
But don't put out the night-light!
Every wise and thoroughly worldly wench
Knows there's always something fishy
about the French!

Refrain 2

BOTH :   Oh, there's always something fishy about
the French!
As a Race, they're conscientious
But undoubtedly licentious,
Tho' the compliments they pay
Are gay
And ever so nice,
We don't believe a word of them.
They may kiss our hands
And talk to us of foreign lands,
We "Toi" and "Moi"
And watch for "Je ne sais quoi."
Every time their fingers begin to clench—
Well, we know there's something fishy
about the French!

After a short dance they go off left as the lights fade.

ACT I

SCENE VII

This Scene is the Public Gardens.

    It is evening, and there are lights in the Pavilion windows.
Down stage on the left is a stone, or wooden seat.
    When the curtain rises there is a mixed collection of people
on the stage. Residents. Visitors. A few soldiers. A
man with a hurdy-gurdy. Several ladies of the town,
some with escorts, some without. Everyone has his back
turned to the audience, and is obviously craning to see
somebody pass by. MISS GOSLETT *and* MISS MENTION,
two elderly maiden ladies, have actually stood upon the
seat in order to see better. After a moment or two, the
tune that the band is playing comes to an end with a little
flourish of brass. Everyone relaxes, and proceeds to
stroll about. MISS GOSLETT *and* MISS MENTION
climb down off the seat and sit on it.

MISS GOSLETT : He's certainly getting very fat.

MISS MENTION : Perhaps it's dropsy.

MISS GOSLETT : Surely not, at his age.

MISS MENTION : A friend of mine died of dropsy when she was only twenty-three. They kept on tapping her and tapping her, but it was no good.

MISS GOSLETT : That poor Princess Caroline, it does seem a shame.

MISS MENTION : Such a common face.

MISS GOSLETT : She can't help that, to be sure.

MISS MENTION : This place is certainly much more lively than Exeter, although I *do* miss the cathedral.

The man with the hurdy-gurdy approaches them, playing busily.

MISS GOSLETT (*fumbling in her reticule*) : I must give him some pence.

MISS MENTION : It will only encourage him.

MISS GOSLETT hands the man a few pennies, and he goes off. The band starts again, this time playing a slightly more sentimental tune. The DUKE OF BENEDEN strolls across accompanied by the MARQUIS OF SHEERE.

EDWARD : But, Papa, I assure you, she is different——

DUKE : My dear boy, that sort of woman is never so very different.

EDWARD (*hotly*) : You cannot possibly tell what sort of woman she is.

DUKE : I shall make it my business to find out.

They go off. SOPHIE walks on accompanied by LORD KENYON, an immaculately dressed dandy, who is obviously a little the worse for drink.

SOPHIE : Not to-night. I have already told you, I have another engagement.

LORD KENYON : Just a little drive.

SOPHIE : I do not trust your horses.

LORD KENYON : What is wrong with them?

SOPHIE : They make conversation impossible.

They meet MARTHA with LORD ST. MARYS.

MARTHA : My dear, I've been searching for you everywhere.

SOPHIE : I can't think why.

MARTHA : Lord St. Marys wants to be presented to Mademoiselle what's-her-name.

SOPHIE (*raising her eyebrows*) : Oh, does he? (*To* LORD

St. Marys.) For your own benefit, or somebody else's?

Lord St. Marys : I cannot give away State secrets.

Sophie : I thought as much.

Martha : I hope this—this commission of yours won't prevent you from coming to the Assembly Rooms later on?

Lord St. Marys : That all depends, neither my heart nor my soul is my own these days——

> *They pass out of sight, all four of them, as the* Duke *of* Beneden *and* Edward *come on right, in time to meet* Lady Julia Charteris *who is strolling down from the back, accompanied only by her maid. She is a handsome authoritative woman, exquisitely gowned, middle-aged, and slightly over made up.*

Duke (*bowing*) : My dear Julia! I thought you were in Spain.

Julia : I'm grateful even for the thought, Frederick. The last ten years have seemed singularly barren without your attentions.

Duke (*hurriedly*) : This is my son, Julia.

Julia (*smiling in response to* Edward's *bow*) : We have met before.

Edward : Madame—I——

Julia : Don't look confused. You couldn't possibly remember. It was years ago, in London. We stopped to converse for a moment, your nurse and I, and you were permitted to bite my glove.

Edward : I never tasted a more delicious glove.

Julia : This has been a strange day, my first in England for a long while. A day of ghosts. Out of the past they come, one after the other, looking almost as real as when they were alive. You are the sixth, Frederick, there really should be seven. Seven is my lucky mumber.

DUKE : You still gamble as much as ever?

JULIA : Yes, with the difference, that I know now that it is far too late to win.

> *They exchange bows. The* DUKE *and* EDWARD *stroll off up stage.* JULIA *has just reached the seat on her way off, when* PAUL *hurries on. He is obviously searching for someone. He passes* JULIA *without looking at her.*

JULIA (*stopping dead*) : The seventh!

PAUL (*turning*) : I beg your pardon?

JULIA (*singing softly*) : Au clair de la lune, mon ami Pierrot——

PAUL (*staring at her*) : Julie!

JULIA : I thought you were dead.

PAUL (*warmly kissing her hands*) : Oh, how charming to see you again, how very, very charming.

JULIA : English, too! Almost without an accent.

PAUL : How long ago is it?

JULIA : Let us both try *not* to remember.

PAUL : It is so difficult——seeing you again so suddenly, so unexpectedly——conjures up so much of the past.

JULIA : The past is dead——perhaps happily.

> *They sit.*

PAUL (*incredulously*) : It isn't true. Do you remember the salon of Madame de Plessier?

JULIA : And Father François, and the little pink cakes with seeds in them——?

PAUL : And the day you cried over the dead dog!

JULIA : I've cried over many dead dogs since then——

> *At this moment* MELANIE *comes on. She goes swiftly up to* PAUL.

MELANIE : Ah, mon cher, enfin! J'ai pensé que vous étiez perdu.

PAUL : Julia, I want to present to you my ward, Melanie de Tramont.

> MELANIE *and* JULIA *both curtsey.* JULIA *is palpably very puzzled.*

JULIA : De *Tramont?*

MELANIE : Oui, Madame. I am the daughter of the dear old Marquis de Tramont.

JULIA : I shouldn't boast of it, my dear, as he was unmarried.

MELANIE (*to* PAUL) : Je ne comprends pas.

PAUL : I will explain later. Lady Julia Charteris and I are very old friends——

> *At this moment*, MARTHA *appears with* LORD ST. MARYS.

MARTHA : Oh, Mademoiselle, will you please allow me to introduce a friend of mine, Lord St. Marys.

> MELANIE *curtseys*, LORD ST. MARYS *bows*.

MELANIE : Enchantée, Monsieur.

LORD ST. MARYS : Please forgive me for imposing myself upon you, Mademoiselle, but I have been commanded to approach you on behalf of His Royal Highness, the Prince Regent.

MELANIE : Ah, mon Dieu! Son Altesse?

LORD ST. MARYS : His Royal Highness wishes to know whether you would do him the honour of taking supper with him this evening?

PAUL : Will you please tell His Royal Highness with our most deep thanks that this evening it would not be possible as she is a little ill.

JULIA : This situation seems a trifle delicate. I hope to continue our reminiscences very soon, Paul. Au revoir, Mademoiselle de Tramont. Come, Hannah.

> *She goes off with her maid.*

51

LORD ST. MARYS : I fear that Mademoiselle does not quite understand. My request, coming from such an exalted quarter, amounts practically to a command.

PAUL : Mademoiselle de Tramont, my ward, has not yet had the honour of being presented to His Royal Highness.

LORD ST. MARYS : The fact, His Royal Highness is the first to deplore——

PAUL : Surely, it is a matter soon remedied?

LORD ST. MARYS : If Mademoiselle will allow me to escort her now, I, myself, will take great pleasure in presenting her.

PAUL : I fear, Monsieur, there is some mistake. Will you kindly bear my homage to His Royal Highness, and inform him, with all due respect, that I will be honoured to present my ward to him myself, on a more formal occasion.

LORD ST. MARYS (*stiffly*) : My regrets, Monsieur.

PAUL (*amiably*) : And mine.

    LORD ST. MARYS *bows abruptly, and goes off with* MARTHA *and* DRAGON *follows.*

MARTHA : Well, really!

PAUL : Come, Melanie.

    He crooks his arm, and MELANIE, *after bowing politely to* MARTHA, *takes it. The band strikes up a particularly gay little tune. As they walk away,* MELANIE *turns her head towards* DRAGON, *who winks broadly at her, kicking up the back of her dress, as——*

THE CURTAIN FALLS

ACT II

Scene I

The painted curtains again.

> Sophie *and* Martha *appear before them as in the*
> *Prologue.*

Sophie : This play, or let us say, this pantomime,
   Being too small in scope, too tenuous,
   Too personal to illustrate the strenuous
   And glittering excitements of the time,
   We feel it, in a sense, obligatory
   To hint at what goes on *behind* the story.

Martha : My friend, though a trifle too rhetorical,
   Means it should be more historical.

Sophie : We ask you to imagine, if you please,
   That just around the corner of the tale,
   Mrs. Fitzherbert and the Prince inhale
   The self-same air, the same urbane sea-
    breeze.
   Imagine that this world is living still
   And passing just beneath the window-sill.

Martha : You've left out Brummell, the pert
    impostor,
   And what about Pitt? And the Duke of
    Gloucester?

Sophie : Picture a little further if you will
   The neat Pavilion Gardens, and the
    Steyne.

The little band that orchestrates the scene.
The Fireworks, the Races, the Quadrille,
And furthermore, the bawdy, merry Hell
Created by our lordly clientèle!
They curtsey and go off, left and right.

ACT II

SCENE II

The Scene is MELANIE'S *room again.*

> *When the curtain rises it is early afternoon.* MELANIE *is seated at a table upon which is a pile of books. She is wearing large horn-rimmed glasses, and an expression of rather depressed concentration. She is also sucking a pencil, and there is a paper bag of humbugs on the table by her side. She sings a song, half in French and half in English, dealing entirely with the intricacies of language. English Lesson:* MELANIE.

Verse

The Tree is in the Garden,
The water is in the Pot;
The Little sheep
On the mountain sleep,
The fire is very hot.

Refrain

Oh! c'est dur,
Tous ces mots obscurs
Me rendent triste;
Rien n'existe
Que le malheur qui insiste;
Dieu, je tâche d'apprendre, mais voilà
Je ne peux pas.

Verse 2

The fire is *not* in the garden,
The tree is not in the pot,
The silly sheep
On the something sleep,
But whether they do or not,
I do not care a jot;
I don't care if they're cold
Or if they're hot.

The CHILDREN *sing,* "La—la—la," *etc., outside the window. She shuts it, and the* CHILDREN *stop singing.*

Refrain 2

Oh! c'est dur,
Tous ces mots obscurs
Me rendent triste;
Rien n'existe
Que le malheur qui insiste;
Dieu, je tâche d'apprendre, mais voilà
Je ne peux pas.

At the end of it, she rests her head wearily on her hands, and is obviously on the verge of tears. ROSE *enters.*

ROSE : There is a lady downstairs to see you.

MELANIE (*perking up slightly*) : Is it Mrs. James or Mrs. Otford?

ROSE : No. She said the name was Lady Julia Charteris.

MELANIE : Tall, with a painted face?

ROSE : Yes, and very grandly dressed. She come in a curricle.

MELANIE : I do not wish to see her. I do not wish to see anyone.

56

Rose : Shall I say you're out?

Melanie : Yes, please—say I am a long way away.

At this moment Lady Julia *comes into the room.*
Melanie *jumps to her feet.*

Julia : Please forgive me, but it was so very draughty in the hall.

Melanie : I am at my work, Madame.

Julia : So I see. How interesting.

Melanie : I fear that Monsieur le Duc is not here.

Julia : I know. It was you I wished to see.

Melanie (*making the best of the situation*) : I am very happy, Madame. Perhaps you will sit yourself?

Julia (*looking round the room*) : Not just for a moment, thank you. I want to enjoy this charming room. What pretty curtains—and what a lovely view.

Melanie : Yes, the view is pretty.

Julia : I believe they are arranging for a new ship to travel between here and Dieppe. That will be so convenient, won't it?

Melanie : I do not very much like ships.

Julia : I have so much to talk to you about. Your guardian and I are old friends, you know. We spent a great deal of our childhood together in France.

Melanie : That is very nice.

Julia : Is it entirely necessary for your maid to chaperon us?

Melanie : You will bring the tea please, Rose.

Rose : Yes, Mademoiselle.

She goes out reluctantly, taking the writing-table.

Julia : It was such a pleasant surprise to see Paul— your guardian—again. I had thought he was dead. (Julia *sits on the sofa.*)

Melanie : No, he is alive.

JULIA : I suppose you are too young to remember his wife, and his mother and father?

MELANIE : Yes, I was young.

JULIA : I understand that you, too, were bereaved of your parents during the Terror.

MELANIE : What, please, is "bereaved"?

JULIA : I mean that they died. That they were guillotined.

MELANIE : Please, I would rather not speak of it.

JULIA : I understand that perfectly. I knew your father many years ago.

MELANIE : Yes?

JULIA : A most witty and delightful man.

MELANIE : Yes, he was very nice.

JULIA : It was so strange of him to keep his marriage such a secret. Paul, apparently, was the only one who knew anything about it.

MELANIE *sits.*

MELANIE : It was a secret because of the Jesuits.

JULIA : The Jesuits?

MELANIE : Yes—my father made them a promise, when he was very little, that he never would take wife and make marriage with himself.

JULIA : I see.

MELANIE : The Jesuits are very powerful.

JULIA : They must be. Where did you live when you were a child?

MELANIE : A grey walled château near Bordeaux. It is all very distant in my mind.

JULIA : The Château de Tramont, no doubt?

MELANIE : Yes. There were swans.

JULIA : Graceful creatures, but disagreeable.

MELANIE : Yes, they were very disagreeable.

JULIA : There was a moat, too, I expect, and tall trees, and I suppose you were brought to Paris by your faithful old nurse?

MELANIE : Yes.

JULIA : You were not dressed as a boy by any chance, were you?

MELANIE : No, why should I be boy?

JULIA : Merely a matter of convention. Perhaps you're really a boy now. Perhaps you're the Dauphin. That's quite an interesting idea.

MELANIE : I think you are laughing.

JULIA : You remember very little about your early life?

MELANIE : It is so far away.

JULIA : So very far away from the truth!

MELANIE (*rising and drawing herself up with great dignity*) : Madame!

JULIA : My dear child, don't be absurd. The whole story is idiotic. You have been very badly rehearsed. Paul should be ashamed of himself.

MELANIE : I do not understand what you speak, Madame.

JULIA : Nonsense. You understand perfectly well.

MELANIE : And I do not understand why you come here.

JULIA : I came to find out what you were like. To see what sort of mistress Paul had picked out for himself.

MELANIE : Mistress! I am no mistress.

JULIA : Oh, come, come, you can hardly expect me to believe that.

MELANIE (*furious*) : How dare you speak these words to me.

JULIA (*rising*) : There is no necessity for you to lose your temper, my dear.

MELANIE : Do not please call me "my dear"—do not please call me any name. Go away.

JULIA : Certainly. I have found out all that I wanted to know.

MELANIE : You have found nothing, because what you know is not true.

JULIA : You can hardly blame me for that, as you have been lying steadily to me for the last ten minutes.

MELANIE : You wish to find about me, do you? You wish to tell all your friends and make a joke. I will explain to you more, very much more. Listen—I am the daughter of a Mandarin in China—he was my first father—my second father was a Russian Jew in Prague—he sold silks, and little jewellery, and furs for your neck—I lived in Spain—I lived in Italy—I was born in the far Indies—my mother was black, black, black! My brothers and sisters were slaves—no, they were little pigs—they ran about in the fields trying with their big noses to find out things—like you, Madame—I am a cocotte from the streets—I am a singer of songs—I am the new wife of Napoleon Bonaparte—take these tales, Madame—take them for your friends—but take them very quickly—now, at this moment—because if you do not go away and leave me alone I will smack your painted face and pull out your dead hair by the roots!

JULIA (*quietly*) : Obviously a guttersnipe.

At this moment PAUL *enters.* MELANIE *runs to him.*
PAUL *and* MELANIE *speak to each other from now on-*
wards in French, unless otherwise indicated.

PAUL : My dear Julia, what a charming surprise—

MELANIE : Dites-lui de s'en aller—elle me rend folle.

PAUL : Mélanie—je vous prie de vous surveiller.

MELANIE : Non, je ne me surveillerai pas. J'en ai assez de me surveiller. J'en ai assez de ces vieilles rosses anglaises. Si elles se regorgent tant, si elles relèvent si haut le nez, c'est sans doute pour ne pas sentir la puanteur de leur fausse moralité. . . .

JULIA : I congratulate you, Paul.

PAUL : My dear Julia——

MELANIE : Appelez-la : ma chère; appelez-la : ma bien-aimée si vous voulez, mais que je ne la voie plus.

PAUL : Lady Julia est une vieille amie, et je ne supporterai pas que vous lui parliez sur ce ton.

MELANIE : Je ne me soucie pas de savoir depuis quand elle est votre amie, mais je sais qu'elle n'a pas le droit de venir ici, chez moi, pour m'insulter.

PAUL : Alors chaque fois que je tourne le dos quelqu'un vous insulte—cela devient fatigant.

MELANIE : C'est pourtant vrai—on m'insulte. Cette vieille bête curieuse m'a jeté à la figure que j'étais votre maîtresse—Je ne le supporterai plus—Je ne resterai pas dans ce pays, pas même pour vous—pas même pour l'amour de Dieu. Je retourne chez les miens—chez les honnêtes et braves gens de la rue—Je n'ai pas besoin de leur mentir à eux—Je n'ai pas besoin d'être polie avec eux, ni de leur faire des sourires, quand j'ai envie de les étrangler—Je vous dis que je retourne en France—Je partirai demain, quand je devrais nager jusque là.

She whirls off into the bedroom and slams the door.
PAUL *and* JULIA *stand looking after her for a moment,*
then JULIA *laughs.*

JULIA : That was all very interesting.

PAUL : I hope, Julia, that since the old days your French has not improved too much.

JULIA : I could understand the gist of what she was saying, if not the actual words.

PAUL : How fortunate.

JULIA : I think, if only on account of our early years, some explanation is required.

PAUL : It was unkind of you to come here and bully the child.

JULIA : I didn't bully her. I merely wanted to find out who and what she was. Then she flew into a strange fury and was extremely rude. I do not like people being rude to me.

PAUL : She shall apologise later on.

JULIA (*grandly*) : That is quite unnecessary.

> ROSE *enters with tea. While she is arranging it upon the table*, JULIA *and* PAUL *talk of other things.*

PAUL : I suppose you have been to the Pavilion?

JULIA : Yes. I supped there the other evening. It is quite hideous.

PAUL : Very informal, I believe?

JULIA : Oh yes, and very agreeable. One plays cards and dances a little. Mrs. Fitzherbert plays very high, but then she always has, hasn't she?

> ROSE *goes out.*

PAUL : It is only by shutting the eyes of my mind very tight that I can conjure up the school-girl I used to know.

JULIA : Surely that is quite natural. Twenty-five years leaves an adequate margin for change—and decay!

PAUL : Decay? (*Sadly.*) Perhaps you are right.

JULIA : Now, tell me, Paul—what does all this mean? Why are you here?

PAUL : It is an odd story, quite fantastic. I think I need you a little.

JULIA : What can I offer you? My heart, my advice, or merely a little tea? (*She goes to the table.*)

PAUL : All three.

JULIA : Surely not the first, when your own is apparently so very much engaged.

PAUL : I fear you misunderstand the situation.

JULIA : I shall be only too pleased to be enlightened. Here is the tea, anyhow. (*She hands him a cup of tea.*)

He stands opposite to her.

PAUL : I feel at a loss—guilty—and yet I have nothing to be guilty about really.

JULIA : I think it was rather unkind of you to take poor Maurice de Tramont's name, and fasten it on to the first little light-of-love you meet.

PAUL *raps his cup sharply on the saucer.*

PAUL (*icily*) : Melanie is not my light-of-love.

JULIA (*smiling incredulously*) : My dear Paul!

PAUL : It's perfectly true. She has never been any-body's light-of-love. That is her greatest asset.

JULIA : Asset?

PAUL (*he sits*) : Yes. Business asset. She is my plan. My trick to be played upon the world. My livelihood.

JULIA : Have you gone mad?

PAUL : No. I have merely transformed myself, owing to hard circumstances, from an effete aristocrat into a cunning and unscrupulous adventurer.

JULIA : That sounds faintly theatrical.

PAUL (*rising*): The murder of my wife and child was theatrical enough—the deaths of my mother and father and sister on the guillotine were equally theatrical. My life from then onwards, as a fugitive, was an endless succession of serio-comic stage effects. I was a baker's assistant—a lawyer's clerk—a tutor to the children of

nouveaux riches parvenus. Two years ago I found
Melanie singing in a café. She seemed to me to be
better material than my snivelling little bourgeois
pupils, so I took her away from the café and kept us
both on my savings. Every now and then I procured
for her an engagement to sing at a private house. Five
months ago I had a stroke of luck. I managed to sell two
pictures from the old house, which somehow or other
had been overlooked by the revolutionaries. With that
money I brought her here.

JULIA : Why?

PAUL : She is to make a rich marriage.

JULIA : And you take commission?

PAUL : Yes.

JULIA : In England, we describe that as pimping!

PAUL : At that rate every fondly ambitious mother is
a pimp.

JULIA : That is hardly the same thing.

PAUL : Well?

JULIA : Well—I think it is a good joke, in very bad
taste.

PAUL : Taste is too expensive a social luxury for a
poor man.

JULIA : I suppose the poor little thing is in love with
you?

PAUL (*startled*) : In love with me! What nonsense.
(*He laughs.*)

JULIA : I should have thought it was inevitable.

PAUL : I appreciate the compliment, Julia, but I
think it is a trifle far-fetched. This whole plan has been
understood completely between us from the first as a
business arrangement.

JULIA : How wise.

64

PAUL : Will you help me?

JULIA : With all your worldly experiences, Paul, you have contrived to remain singularly naïf.

PAUL : At any rate, even if you cannot help, please make me a promise that you will not hinder.

JULIA : Of course if it's money you want you could always marry me. I have plenty.

PAUL (*shocked*) : Julia!

JULIA : We could find some employment for Melanie. She might even be my maid.

PAUL : I see I have made a mistake.

JULIA (*rising with decision, and patting his shoulder*) : No, Paul. Don't be afraid. I won't give away your secret, and I'll help you all I can. It should be amusing at least.

PAUL : How much do you despise me for it?

JULIA : Just a little. If it matters to you.

PAUL : I'm sorry.

JULIA : Cunning, unscrupulous adventurers have no time to waste on conscience. Call her in. We will discuss possibilities.

PAUL : Do you think that is wise?

JULIA : I can manage her.

PAUL : Very well. (*He goes to the bedroom door.*) Melanie. Venez ici.

After a moment MELANIE *comes in. She sees that* JULIA *is still there and her face hardens immediately.*

PAUL : Melanie. I wish you to apologise to Lady Julia.

MELANIE (*firmly*) : No.

PAUL (*sternly*) : Please do as I tell you.

MELANIE : I have nothing to say.

JULIA : But it is for me to say I am sorry. I was over-

65

inquisitive and I jumped to conclusions too hastily. Mademoiselle, I ask your forgiveness.

MELANIE (*bowing*) : Merci, Madame.

JULIA : Shall we be friends?

MELANIE : Je ne comprends pas.

PAUL : You are being very ungracious, Melanie.

MELANIE : I am sorry.

PAUL : I have told Lady Julia everything. She has promised to help us.

MELANIE : You have told her—what?

JULIA : A story. Just a story, Mademoiselle, but it is a very interesting story, and I should like, as Paul and I are such old friends, to help to bring it to a happy ending.

> MELANIE *looks searchingly from one to the other, and then, with a great effort, smiles.*

MELANIE (*curtseying*) : Merci beaucoup, Madame. I understand now.

> JULIA *also curtseys.*

JULIA (*briskly*) : Come now—to business.

MELANIE (*with great manner*) : Madame will sit?

JULIA (*sitting down*) : Thank you.

MELANIE (*enquiringly to* PAUL) : What business shall we begin?

PAUL : We can talk quite freely in front of Lady Julia.

MELANIE : That is very nice.

JULIA : In the first place, whom do you know here?

MELANIE (*humming softly*) : Even the sea looks grey.

PAUL : Melanie!

MELANIE (*fiercely singing*) : C'est vrai!

JULIA (*politely*) : I beg your pardon?

MELANIE : It is nothing, Madame, but when business

is here to be talked—— (*Singing.*) It seems that all the joy has faded from the day—as though the foolish world no longer wants to play——

JULIA : Really, these vocal outbursts are most disconcerting.

PAUL : Do be good, Melanie.

MELANIE : Very well—I will be good.

PAUL : Lord Sheere is our only definite proposal so far.

JULIA (*to* MELANIE) : Do you like him?

MELANIE (*singing*) :

> I'll follow my secret heart my whole life
> through.
> I'll keep every dream apart till one comes
> true.
> No matter what price is paid,
> What stars may fade—above
> I'll follow my secret heart
> Till I find—Love.

She rises while she is singing this, and walks over to the window. She finishes with her back turned.

PAUL (*irritably*) : Melanie! Will you kindly concentrate?

JULIA : I do see how difficult it must be, for anyone so young and so charming, to banish sentiment entirely.

MELANIE (*turning*) : You are sympathetic, Madame, but it is not so very difficult really. Sentiment is very silly. (*She looks at* PAUL *and her voice hardens.*)

JULIA : How wise.

MELANIE : There is no sentiment in the whole world that is real.

JULIA : Wiser still.

MELANIE : Real enough to waste the time upon— Paul has spoken me that very often.

JULIA : How very sensible of him.

MELANIE : I will be sensible too and make business. (*She puts a chair by the table and sits.*) I have three with which to begin.

JULIA : Three!

MELANIE : Yes, I make the progress. First there is the Prince Regent. He wishes to sleep with me.

PAUL : Melanie!

MELANIE (*quickly*) : Do not be shocked, Paul. That is true, and we are speaking of truth.

JULIA (*laughing*) : Admirable.

MELANIE : If I do that—there is a risk—a risk that I may not stay in the royal heart long enough to gain large money for Paul.

PAUL : I will not have you speaking like that—it is intolerable.

JULIA : She is quite right, Paul. It ill becomes you to be so outraged. Remember how unscrupulous you are.

MELANIE : Then there is the Duke of Beneden. He has a little house with pretty furniture and a coach with brown horses and three hundred pounds on the first day of every month—these things would be useful, would they not?

JULIA : Hard work, but a little more lasting than the other.

MELANIE : Then there is Lord Sheere.

JULIA : That's better.

MELANIE : He loves me.

JULIA : Excellent.

MELANIE : But if we marry, there is no money at all.

JULIA : That can soon be remedied if your social position is improved. You must first of all be presented —more or less informally, here—at the Pavilion.

PAUL : But how? Who will present her?

JULIA : I will, but before that you must give a little supper party. I will arrange it, and invite the guests. Lord St. Marys must come, and the Benedens, and Lord Sheere, and the Harringfords—they are very useful.

MELANIE (*rising sharply*) : Are they rich? Have they a foolish son? (*She goes to the window.*)

JULIA (*ignoring her, to* PAUL) : You must have cards, and good wine—Mademoiselle might sing a little—she has such a charming voice, but I should suggest songs more closely allied to the Classics than to the café chantant.

PAUL (*going over to her*) : I can never begin to express my gratitude, Julia——

JULIA : Not at all. Old friends must be kept from starving. If all else fails I shall take up a subscription for you.

PAUL : I am still very low in your eyes, I see.

JULIA : You share that position with almost everyone I know. (*Rising.*) I will leave you now. Call upon me to-morrow and we will discuss the party invitations.

PAUL : I will send for a carriage.

JULIA : My curricle is outside. (*She crosses to* MELANIE *and curtseys.*) Au revoir, Mademoiselle.

MELANIE : Au revoir, Madame.

JULIA : And please accept my admiration. Your common sense is magnificent—(*she laughs*). But you will be careful, won't you, not to betray too much hardness of heart. Cynicism in the young is *so* unbecoming.

> *She sweeps out, followed by* PAUL. MELANIE, *when they have gone, picks up* JULIA'S *handkerchief from the floor, sniffs it contemptuously, and pitches it into the waste-paper basket—as the lights fade.*

ACT II

SCENE III

QUARTETTE : FISHERMEN.
" There was once a little village."

There was once a little village by the sea,
Where we lived our lives in amiable tranquillity.
We were humble in our ways
And we swam through all our days
As little fishes swim—in immobility ;
We watched for gales in the evening sky
And we trimmed our sails till the night went by,
No less, no more,
Than stones on an English shore.

Then whimsical Fate,
Resenting our state,
Decided to break us
And mould and re-make us ;
Our sweet isolation
From civilisation
Has all vanished away.
We're urban and proud,
Supporting a crowd
Of Doxys and Dandys
And Regency Randys,
Who fiddle and faddle
And piddle and paddle

70

And turn night into day.
The Pavilion
Cost a million
As a monument to Art,
And the wits here
Say it sits here
Like an Oriental tart !
The dashing " beau monde "
Has ruffled our pond,
And even the turbot
Know Mrs. Fitzherbert.
We're richer than ever before
But Brighton is Brighton no more.

ACT II

SCENE IV

The Scene is a larger room on the ground floor of MELANIE'S
*house. It is circular and the ceiling is supported by
pillars. There are two sets of double doors upstage
right and left. Downstage, almost on the footlights,
there are two curved benches. There is a buffet on the
left side of the stage upon which are jugs of iced wine
and elaborate cakes and other delicacies. From behind
the right hand double doors comes the sound of music.
There are candles on the buffet, and in sconces on the
walls.   Hanging in the centre is a large crystal chandelier.
Up at the back of the stage between the door there is a
low dais upon which is a clavisan.*

When the CURTAIN *rises the* GUESTS *are grouped, with*
JULIA *and* PAUL *in the centre, forming a beautiful
" still " picture. This attitude is held through a phrase
of music, when, at a given point, the " picture " comes
to life, and the party is in progress.*

*Note :   Throughout this Scene there are musical
" stops " to allow the dialogue to be heard.   All guests,
etc., not actually concerned in dialogue, remain immovable,
in whichever positions they may be.*

*There is the sound of laughter and dancing from the
ballroom.*   GUESTS *are strolling about and chatting to
one another.   There are several people clustered round
the buffet.*

72

PAUL *and* JULIA *are standing centre. A* BUTLER
flings open the doors left, and announces, in succession :

BUTLER : Lady Mosscrock. The Earl and Countess
of Harringford.

The HARRINGFORDS *enter and* PAUL *goes forward
to receive them. The conversation is too general for
their exact greetings to be heard. They come over to*
JULIA *and talk for a little, meanwhile the* BUTLER
announces in succession, MR. *and* MRS. HAILSHAM,
THE LADY BRACEWORTH, THE HONOURABLE
JULIAN KANE, LORD DOYNING. (*Musical stop.*)

LADY H. (*to* JULIA) : What a charming house, and
what a lovely party. You must come to tea to-morrow
and tell me the name of our host over and over again.
I know I shall never remember it.

JULIA : The Duc de Chaucigny-Varennes.

LADY H. : The French do seem to go out of their
way to make things hard for us, don't they ?   All those
hyphens.

LORD H. : Where's the girl you told us about ?   The
ward or niece or whatever she is.

JULIA : You shall see her soon.   She is very lovely.

Music resumes.

They pass on to talk to someone else. The BUTLER
announces THE DUKE *and* DUCHESS *OF* BENEDEN.
When they enter PAUL *receives them politely but with
a certain hauteur. Presently the* DUCHESS *takes*
JULIA'S *arm and walks her downstage left. They sit
for a few moments on the curved bench.* (*Musical stop.*)

DUCHESS : Julia.   I must tell you frankly.   I do not
understand at all.   I am completely at a loss.

JULIA : Why, Georgina ?

DUCHESS : Frederick made me come, I still don't approve——

JULIA : You have no reason not to approve. You merely jumped to conclusions too hastily. As usual.

DUCHESS : Do you mean to tell me——

JULIA : I don't mean to tell you anything, Georgina, except that I have known the Chaucigny-Varennes family all my life, and that Paul is one of my oldest friends.

DUCHESS : But the girl—I can't believe——

JULIA : You made a grave mistake, and all I can suggest is that you remedy it as soon as possible. Melanie will be down soon.

The DUKE *joins them.*

DUKE : Is Edward here ?

JULIA : I haven't seen him yet.

DUCHESS: He hasn't spoken to me for four days.

JULIA : You really can't be surprised. You both of you made a bad blunder.

DUCHESS : But those dreadful women ! Trying on each other's hats.

JULIA : Melanie is a stranger here. How was she to know whom to receive and whom not to receive ?

DUCHESS : Very well, Julia, I'll take your word for it, for the time being, but I'm still not convinced.

Music resumes—Short phrase—Musical stop.

She moves away to talk to LADY HARRINGFORD.

JULIA : Really, Frederick, Georgina is more disagreeable than ever.

DUKE : She is upset.

JULIA : You've been saying that for twenty years.

DUKE : It's been true for twenty years.

JULIA : I don't know how you've stood it.

74

DUKE: On the contrary, you should know better than anyone.

JULIA (*laughing*): Yes, Frederick, perhaps I should. Poor Georgina.

DUKE: The years have changed you very little.

JULIA: Thank you, Frederick.

DUKE: Dear Julia. (*He kisses her hand.*)

JULIA: That gesture was reminiscent—almost painfully so. Fortunately the light is too strong to allow us to deceive ourselves.

DUKE: Deceive ourselves?

JULIA: Into a momentary belief that we were young again.

DUKE: Julia—do you remember——?

JULIA: I remember nothing. That is one of my greatest virtues. Who is your mistress at the moment?

DUKE: Really, Julia!

JULIA: Or have you retired from public love?

(*Music resumes.*)

She curtseys to him rather mockingly, and goes over to PAUL. *The* DUKE *moves over to the buffet. There is a general buzz of conversation during which* LORD SHEERE *and* LORD ST. MARYS *are announced and make their entrance.* PAUL *receives them.*

(*Musical stop.*)

MELANIE *comes in quite quietly and unostentatiously, but even so, her entrance is the signal for the conversation to die down. People turn, with elaborate casualness, to scrutinize her. She looks pale, but very lovely.*

MELANIE (*to* PAUL): My dress would not manage itself. I am so sorry. (*She curtseys to* JULIA.) Madame.

JULIA: You look delicious, my dear.

MELANIE: Merci, Madame.

75

She curtseys to EDWARD *and* LORD ST. MARYS.

JULIA (*to the* DUCHESS OF BENEDEN): Georgina—I want to present to you Mademoiselle Melanie de Tramont.

DUCHESS (*stiffly*): How do you do?

MELANIE (*curtseying low*): I am honoured, Madame.

DUCHESS (*with an effort*): I am delighted to see you again.

MELANIE: Again? Ah, forgive me, Madame, but I am so quite sure that we have never, never met before.

DUCHESS: That is very charming of you, Mademoiselle.

The DUKE *comes up.*

PAUL: Ah, Monsieur le Duc, I wish to present my ward, Melanie de Tramont.

The DUKE *bows low, and again* MELANIE *curtseys.*

DUKE: I hope you are enjoying yourself in England, Mademoiselle?

MELANIE: Yes, I love it here. The sea is so pretty!
(*Music resumes.*)
(*Musical stop.*)

The BUTLER *flings open the doors and announces,* MRS. JAMES, MRS. OTFORD *and* MRS. DRAGON. *There is a horrified silence for a moment or two.*

PAUL: Melanie! Did you invite them?

MELANIE: Pourquoi pas? They are my friends.

SOPHIE *and* MARTHA *enter, followed discreetly by* MRS. DRAGON. *They are extravagantly dressed and over-bejewelled.*

SOPHIE: My dear, what a *lovely* party.

MARTHA: So sweet of you to ask us.

They curtsey. MELANIE *greets them with enthusiasm.*

JULIA (*to* PAUL): This is idiotic!

PAUL : We must get rid of them.

JULIA : It's too late now. Oh, what an abysmal mistake !

DUCHESS (*to* PAUL, *sweetly*) : Good night, Monsieur. It has been so delightful.

PAUL : But surely, Duchess, you are not leaving ?

DUCHESS : A sudden headache. It will be better in the morning. My husband, I am sure, will be delighted to stay.

> *She bows coldly to* JULIA *and goes out.* LADY
> HARRINGFORD *comes up to* PAUL.

LADY H. : Good night, Monsieur—I have to drive to London early to-morrow and I am very tired.

> (*Music resumes.*)
>
> PAUL *bows, and she goes off after the* DUCHESS.
>
> *Nearly all the women in the room come up in turn to say good-bye to* PAUL, *but you do not hear the exact excuses they give because* MELANIE *has led* SOPHIE *and* MARTHA *and* MRS. DRAGON *downstage right to the bench.*
>
> (*Musical stop.*)

JULIA (*to* PAUL) : You see ! (*She sits.*)

SOPHIE : We should scold you, Melanie.

MELANIE : What is "scold" ?

MARTHA : Be angry.

MELANIE : Angry ! Why ?

SOPHIE : We didn't know it was this sort of party.

MELANIE : I do not understand.

SOPHIE : We never like meeting these sort of women.

MARTHA : Most of them are the wives of our gentlemen, you know. It's very awkward.

SOPHIE : Don't stand there twiddling your fingers, Dragon. Go and get yourself some claret.

MRS. DRAGON *goes over to the buffet.*

MELANIE (*noticing what is happening*): They have all gone away—all the ladies.

SOPHIE: That's our fault.

MELANIE (*suddenly angry*): I understand now—very, very well—Paul——

PAUL *comes over to her.*

Paul—I do not believe you know Madame Otford and Madame James.

PAUL (*bowing coldly*): Enchanted.

MELANIE: These ladies have been very kind to me— I should like that you know that—they have made me happy——

PAUL: That is delightful.

SOPHIE: I think we had better go, Martha. I feel quite faint.

MELANIE: If you go, I will go with you.

PAUL: Don't be ridiculous, Melanie.

MELANIE (*to* SOPHIE): You must not go—you must stay for me to sing—it is all arranged—Lord Sheere— Lord St. Marys——

EDWARD *and* LORD ST. MARYS *come over to her.*

PAUL: Melanie!

MELANIE: This is my party, Paul. I wish to enjoy myself. Lord Sheere, Lord St. Marys—I have something to say to you—where is the Duke?—I have something to say to him also.

JULIA (*rising*): What is happening?

MELANIE: Nothing, Madame, except that I am going to sing—it was planned that I should sing—because I sing so charmingly, do I not? (*To* EDWARD *and* LORD ST. MARYS.) Messieurs, you will sit, please, next to my two friends—ah, Monsieur le Duc de Beneden—I

wish that you pay very special favour to a lady much
in my esteem—Mrs. Dragon——

> *She darts to the buffet and brings* MRS. DRAGON
> *over to the* DUKE. MRS. DRAGON *looks slightly
> flustered owing to having a glass of claret in one hand
> and a large sandwich in the other. However, she
> manages to curtsey, a trifle unsteadily.*

Where is Mr. Jones ? He is to play—please find Mr.
Jones, Paul——

JULIA (*laughing, none too pleasantly*): Excellent—the
whole situation is most entertaining.

MELANIE : I am glad if you are gay, Madame—I
would like that everybody is gay.

PAUL (*to* MELANIE): Melanie—écoutez ! Je veux
vous dire quelque chose d'importance——

MELANIE : Do not speak in French, Paul—I cannot
understand—I can understand only English among my
English friends—ah, there is Mr. Jones—please play
for me, Mr. Jones—Mr. Jones plays very light, very
pretty—everybody will please sit—Monsieur le Marquis
—it is from the distance that you see me now—please
for me remember that—Monsieur le Duc—when you
are in your small house in London, with the shutters
drawn—think sweetly of me, because I shall be far
away—Lord St. Marys, you have proposed such kind
honours, but I am too little in life to say Yes or No—
I may only say merci——

> MR. JONES *begins to play the clavisan. Everybody
> sits down, looking faintly bewildered.* PAUL *remains
> standing, near* JULIA. MELANIE *starts to sing. First
> she sings to* EDWARD, *briefly, but with very genuine
> sweetness. Then she turns to the* DUKE OF BENEDEN.
> For him, the words she sings are tinged with gentle*

79

malice.   She sings to LORD ST. MARYS *smilingly and with a certain mocking deference.   Last of all she turns suddenly towards* PAUL.   *To him she sings in French, an unmistakable love song.   Her whole heart is in her voice.* PAUL *starts back in horrified amazement.* JULIA'S *face hardens into an expression of ill-repressed fury.*

(*Musical Finale.*)

MELANIE : Dear Friends,
    Will you forgive me, pray,
    If many of the words I say
    In English may be wrong.

ALL : She hasn't been in England very long.

MELANIE : A stranger in a foreign land,
    I beg that you will understand
    How gratefully I find
    The gentlemen so very kind,
    So very kind.

  (*To the* DUKE OF BENEDEN.)
    The offer of protection
    That Monsieur le Duc has made
    I set aside,
    For my foolish pride
    Would feel itself betrayed.

ALL : Charming—Charming—Charming !

MELANIE (*to* LORD ST. MARYS) :
    Monsieur, my Lord St. Marys
    Has made me an offer too.
    Royal though his scheme may be,
    It could never be part of a dream for me.

ALL : Ah la la la—la la—la la.

MELANIE : Handsome though your Prince may be,
    He is far too broad in the beam for me.

(*To the* MARQUIS OF SHEERE.)

> But there is one, one only,
> Who honours me with his heart,
> Although I'm not the wife for him
> I shall cherish all my life for him
> A feeling somehow apart.
> I'd suffer sorrow and strife for him.
> Though we may be lovers never,
> We're friends for ever—for evermore.

(*Spoken.*)

Thank you, my dear, for being so sweet to me.

EDWARD (*kissing her hand*): Melanie!

MELANIE: There is only room for one true love in my heart—my secret heart.

EDWARD: I understand.

MELANIE: I know you do.

JULIA: This is most illuminating.

MELANIE: Paul!

PAUL (*horrified*): Melanie—please——

MELANIE (*simply*): It is you I love, I always have, from the very beginning——   (*She sings.*)

> C'est assez de mensonge,
> Le secret qui me ronge,
> Que tout au fond de moi
> J'ai tendrement gardé.
> Enfin avec franchise
> Il faut que je vous dise,
> Avouant mon secret,
> Que tu n'as pas compris
> Plus de cœur discret,
> C'est toi qui par l'amour,
> Toi qui m'as délivrée,
> Je suis à toi toujours.

81

Esclave de mon cœur,
Me rendras-tu la vie.
Je t'en supplie, crois-moi,
Lorsque je dis c'est toi
Plus de cœur discret.
C'est toi qui par l'amour,
Toi qui m'as délivrée,
Je suis à toi toujours.
Esclave de mon cœur,
Me rendras-tu la vie.
Je t'en supplie, crois-moi,
Je t'en supplie, crois-moi,
C'est Toi.
Parmi le monde entier c'est toi que j'aime.
Je t'en supplie,
Crois-le si même
Tu ne le veux.
Toi,
Parmi le monde entier c'est toi que j'aime,
Je suis à toi Toujours.

At the end of the song MELANIE *swoons. There is an immediate buzz of excited conversation.* SOPHIE *runs forward, followed by* MARTHA. LORD ST. MARYS *hurries forward with a chair.*

SOPHIE : Dragon—fetch some wine—quickly——

MARTHA : Feathers—burn them under her nose—here—— (*She tears some feathers out of her hair.*)

SOPHIE : That's no good.

JULIA : A strange performance.

PAUL (*quivering*) : Please go now—I wish that every-one should go.

All the men start to go.

JULIA : Very well—poor Paul—I am so sorry.

82

PAUL : To-morrow—we will talk to-morrow.

JULIA : Frederick !—Edward—will you please see me to my carriage ?

> JULIA *and the* DUKE *exeunt.*

SOPHIE (*to* MELANIE) : It's all right, dear—we're all going——

MELANIE (*opening her eyes*) : Paul.

MARTHA : Just lie still a minute.

SOPHIE : Come away, Martha.

MARTHA : All right, all right, I'm coming——

> *They go to the door, call* DRAGON *and all go out.*
> *During this scene nearly everyone has gone.* MELANIE
> *is sitting on a chair, very white and quite still.* PAUL
> *sees the last guest,* EDWARD, *out, and closes the door.*

PAUL (*in a cold voice*) : Well—I hope you're satisfied.

MELANIE (*pleadingly*) : Paul !

PAUL : Everything is ruined—everything is finished.

MELANIE : Je vous aime.

PAUL : Ne vous moquez pas de moi.

MELANIE : Non, c'est vrai. Je vous ai toujours aimé.

PAUL : Vous avez d'étranges façons de me témoigner votre amour ; en me rendant ridicule.

MELANIE : Est-ce si ridicule d'être aimé de moi ?

PAUL : Il ne peut pas y avoir d'amour entre nous ; une folie—voilà tout.

MELANIE : Non, c'est vrai.

PAUL : Savez-vous seulement ce qui est vrai ? Vous avez manqué à tous vos engagements, vous m'avez menti, vous êtes jouée de moi.

> *Angrily he crosses to the sofa* L.

MELANIE : Et pourquoi m'en serais-je privée ? Dans toutes vos adroites combinaisons avez-vous un seul instant—pensé—à moi ? Jamais !

PAUL : Pardon—tout était convenu entre nous dès le début.   Vous saviez tout et vous aviez tout accepté.

MELANIE : Bien sûr, j'avais tout accepté.   Une fille dans la situation où j'étais, aurait été folle de ne pas tout accepter.

PAUL : C'était un contrat d'affaires, et vous y avez manqué.

MELANIE : Pouvais-je répondre de mon cœur ?

PAUL : De votre cœur !

MELANIE : Je vous aime, vous entendez. Vous pouvez dire que je suis folle, vous pouvez vous persuader que tout ceci est stupidement romanesque : cela vous met à votre aise, n'est-ce pas ?

PAUL : Je suis parfaitement à mon aise.

MELANIE : Mais c'est vrai, et mon amour est au fond de moi, au plus profond de moi.   De ma vie, aucun sentiment n'a poussé en moi des racines si profondes. Regardez-moi   maintenant—regardez-moi   bien !—je vous en prie, vous qui êtes si sage et si stupidement cruel—vous—l'homme le plus adroit que je connaisse et, de loin, le plus imbécile.

PAUL : Merci !

MELANIE :   Vous   avez   pour   toujours   renoncé à l'amour, quand votre femme a été tuée, n'est-ce pas ?   Dieu merci, vous me l'avez assez souvent répété.

PAUL : Melanie, je vous en prie !

MELANIE : Et alors vous pensez pouvoir traverser la vie à l'abri, inaccessible, dans une magnifique sécurité, n'est-ce pas ?

PAUL : Je me passerai fort bien de vos conseils.

MELANIE : Vous m'avez ramassée dans le ruisseau

et vous m'avez appris la révérence et à faire les manières et à mentir à la vie.

PAUL : C'était bien nécessaire.

MELANIE : Mais voilà que, tout à coup, la vie a pris sa revanche, et elle s'est jouée de vous—et elle s'en jouera toujours. La vie est trop puissante en moi pour que j'accepte vos combinaisons. C'est vrai la vie—et c'est important—plus important que votre tranquillité et que votre cynisme prudent.

PAUL : Vous perdez le sens.

MELANIE : Allez-vous-en, et réfléchissez un peu. Allez-vous-en, et comprenez brusquement quel mal infini vous avez essayé de me faire.

PAUL : C'en est trop !

MELANIE : —et à vous aussi——

PAUL : C'en est trop !

MELANIE : —je t'aime—je t'aime—je t'aime—et toi aussi quelque part au fond de toi—tu m'aimes.

PAUL *starts to go.*

Tout me le crie. Chacun de mes instincts, chaque battement de mon cœur, chaque bouffée d'air que je respire. Vous allez essayer de m'échapper—cela aussi je le sais—mais vous ne le pourrez pas——

He is just going out of the door and she breaks down completely.

—vous ne le pourrez pas——

She sinks into the chair, sobbing. The last chords of her love song to him crash out in the orchestra as—

THE CURTAIN FALLS

ACT III

Scene I

The Scene is " The Steyne " and the time of day is about noon. It is a clear sunny morning and there are a good many people strolling about. As usual, there is an undercurrent of music to the whole scene, and Characters pass as in the First Act.

Miss Goslett and Miss Mention walk slowly across, talking.

Miss Goslett : You don't put the nutmeg on until afterwards.

Miss Mention : I still don't understand. Surely if you leave it too long to cool, it gets lumpy.

Miss Goslett : Not if you stir it enough in the first place.

Miss Mention : And why a *wooden* spoon ?

Miss Goslett : It says so in the recipe.

Miss Mention : Well, personally I prefer to remain faithful to the ordinary tapioca.

They both pass out of sight.

The Lady Braceworth enters right with the Duchess of Beneden. They meet Mrs. Hailsham centre, who has come on from the left.

Duchess : Good morning, Amelia.

Mrs. Hailsham : My dear. (*They kiss.*)

Lady B. : Amelia.

Mrs. Hailsham : My dear. (*They kiss.*)

86

DUCHESS : How is Mortimer ?

MRS. HAILSHAM : Worse, I'm afraid. He had a shivering fit at three this morning. I've been up half the night.

LADY B. : How dreadful !

MRS. HAILSHAM : When he crept into my bed at about six he seemed calmer, but his nose was very hot and dry.

DUCHESS : You really should take him to the Vet.

MRS. HAILSHAM : I intend to this afternoon.

LADY HARRINGFORD *joins them.*

LADY H. : Georgina.

DUCHESS : Ettie. (*They kiss.*)

LADY H. : Amelia !

LADY B. : Good morning, Ettie. (*They kiss.*)

LADY H. : Louisa !

MRS. HAILSHAM : My dear. (*They kiss.*)

LADY H. : I've had a horrible morning. Nono was sick three times at breakfast.

DUCHESS : Perhaps it's an epidemic.

LADY H. : I shall take him to the Vet. this afternoon.

LADY B. : Is he a really good Vet. ?

MRS. HAILSHAM : Charming, my dear, absolutely charming.

LADY B. : Then I shall come with you this afternoon and bring Fifi.

DUCHESS : Is she ill too ?

LADY B. : Well, not exactly ill, but moody.

LADY H. : There's probably something in the air here, it's very strong.

DUCHESS : Funnily enough it seems to suit Boney very well. He's much brighter here than in Shropshire.

MRS. HAILSHAM : Shropshire *is* enervating.

DUCHESS : I can't decide whether it's the sea air or the sulphur tablets, but he's certainly a different dog.

LADY B. : I'm so glad, because I never cared for him very much as he was.

DUCHESS : It betrays a small mind, Louisa, to be offended just because he didn't take to you at the very first moment.

MRS. HAILSHAM : I don't like animals to be too friendly.

DUCHESS : At any rate he is a remarkably good house-dog.

LADY B. : I should say more thorough than good.

DUCHESS : Really, Louisa !

MRS. HAILSHAM : How is Frederick ?

DUCHESS : I really don't know, he didn't come home until four.

LADY H. : Neither did James.

MRS. HAILSHAM : Nor Robert.

LADY B. : Desmond hasn't come home yet.

LADY H. : It's such a bad example for the children. They ask such difficult questions.

DUCHESS : That dreadful party, and those appalling women.   I shall never forgive Julia.

LADY B. : She must be mad.

LADY H. : The French Duke seemed polite, I thought, but peculiar.

MRS. HAILSHAM : My dear, (*to music*) there's always something fishy about the French.

DUCHESS : As a race they're erotic.

LADY B. : And completely idiotic.

LADY H. : Still, they have a certain air.

MRS. HAILSHAM: A " flair."

DUCHESS: Whatever you say, I don't believe a word of it.

They all talk together.

MRS. HAILSHAM: I didn't object to the girl so much, of course she was quite obviously common——

LADY B.: It's all very fine to excuse them on the grounds of being foreigners, but really——

LADY H.: Never in all my life have I had such a shock as when the door opened and those women came into the room——

DUCHESS: It's entirely Julia's fault. She gave me her solemn promise that she had known the Duke for years——

On the last phrase of " Fishy about the French," which the orchestra has been playing softly during this scene, they all sing suddenly together.

ALL FOUR: There's *always* something fishy about the French !

This last line leads them into their quartette, " Mothers and Wives," during which SOPHIE, MARTHA, MRS. DRAGON *and another courtesan trip gaily across the scene on the arms of the* DUKE OF BENEDEN, MR. HAILSHAM, LORD BRACEWORTH *and* LORD HARRINGFORD.

QUARTETTE: "MOTHERS AND WIVES."

In an atmosphere of bawdy jeu d'esprit
We contrive to be tenaciously conventional,
Tho' intelligent, we hope,
Our imaginative scope
When all is said and done
Is one-dimensional.

Our appearance should be ample guarantee
Of our vigorous and rigorous morality,
We regard our husbands' gout
As a proper and devout
And Godly recompense
For sensuality.
But when we look at our greying hairs
We sometimes sigh as we say our prayers,
Dear Lord,
We're bored,
Is virtue enough reward?

Finally, at the end of the quartette, the mothers and wives go disconsolately away, leaving the stage comparatively empty save for a few pedestrians who pass and re-pass from time to time. JULIA *and* PAUL *enter from the left. During this scene, characters pass by at given moments.*

JULIA : My dear Paul, such sentimentality is utterly ridiculous.

PAUL : That is how I feel.

JULIA : Those feelings may do credit to your heart, but certainly not to your intelligence.

PAUL : It has nothing to do with my heart.

JULIA : Are you sure?

PAUL (*vehemently*) : Quite sure.

JULIA : Then be sensible. This idiotic charade cannot go on any further, you must see that.

PAUL : Yes, I see that.

JULIA : She is a nice little thing and, I am sure, perfectly sincere, but as is only to be expected, when a girl of her class is suddenly plumped down in an entirely different milieu, her values have become hopelessly confused.

PAUL : How can I send her away ?   She has done her best.

JULIA : It was a business contract between you, and now it is over.

PAUL : I know, but——

JULIA : She made a fool of you last night.   She took your pride from you, and your position from you, and those are all that you have left.

PAUL : Not intentionally.

JULIA : Look at me for a moment, Paul, carefully and clearly.   I am middle-aged and lonely and, oddly enough, I love you.

PAUL : Julia !

JULIA : Don't affect such surprise.   You must know it perfectly well.   You must have known that I would not have taken all this trouble to help you with a scheme of which I heartily disapproved if I had not realised, in the first moment of seeing you again, that over all these years, and through all our strange adventures, you are the one man in the whole world that I love, and that I have always loved.

PAUL : What can I say to you, Julia ?

JULIA : The truth, whatever it may be.

PAUL : I don't believe I know it.

JULIA (*smiling*) : Dear Paul.

PAUL : Are you laughing at me ?

JULIA : Just a little.

PAUL : I am sure you are right to laugh, but please don't, I feel small enough already, and cheap, and of no account.

JULIA : You are worrying about Melanie ?

PAUL : Of course.

JULIA : Listen to me.   She is not happy here, she

never has been. We will send her back to Paris with enough money to keep her in comfort until she finds a nice husband for herself of her own class.

PAUL: I have no money.

JULIA: I have, a lot.

PAUL: Julia!

JULIA: Please, please, I beseech you to be sensible. Money cannot matter between us, just as the wild ecstasies of passion cannot matter between us. I am rich and, as I said before, lonely. You are poor, and equally lonely. We have still time for many years of happiness together—Paul——

She knocks at the door.

PAUL: If only I could have known before.

JULIA: Fate has offered us a wonderful chance. It would be foolish to allow it to slip away.

PAUL: Perhaps you are right—perhaps this is the truth.

JULIA: The truth is here, very clear and simple. Two very old friends have suddenly, unaccountably, found each other again——

She holds out her hand to him and he kisses it. During this scene all the lights have faded except on the exact spot where they are standing. As JULIA turns to go into the house, this light also fades.

ACT III

Scene II

The Scene is Melanie's *room again.*

When the Curtain rises Melanie *and* Edward *are discovered clasped tightly in each other's arms. They do not move until* Rose *enters.*

Rose : Mademoiselle.

Melanie (*over* Edward's *shoulder*) : Yes ?

Rose : It was only the milkman.

Melanie (*irritably*) : Oh—— (*To* Edward.) Then we will sit down again.

Rose : Do you want some fresh chocolate ?

Melanie (*feeling the chocolate pot on the table*) : No, this is still quite hot.

Rose *goes out.*

Edward : I think I should like a little.

Melanie (*pouring it out*) : Here—— (*She motions him to sit.*) There is a little cake, too, if you would care.

Edward : No, thank you.

Melanie (*eating one*) : They are delicious.

Edward : Very well, I will try one. (*He takes a cake.*)

Melanie : What will we speak of ?

Edward : I don't know.

Melanie (*smiling*) : You are so very sweet.

Edward : I don't think we will speak of that, anyhow.

MELANIE : And very, very kind.

EDWARD : No, really I'm not.

MELANIE : And my very, very good friend.

EDWARD : I hope so.   I do hope so.

MELANIE : Would you have another small cake ?

EDWARD : Yes, please.

MELANIE : I will also.

They both have another cake.

MELANIE : In Paris there are very lovely cakes.

EDWARD : There must be.

There is a rat-tat-tat at the front door.   They both put their chocolate cups down hurriedly.

MELANIE : Quickly.

EDWARD : I say, my mouth's full.

MELANIE : Never mind—so is mine.

They fly into each other's arms and stand motionless. Presently ROSE *re-enters.*

ROSE : It's only the girl from Mrs. Baxter's, with a bill.

MELANIE : Send her away.

ROSE : I have.

She goes out.

MELANIE (*going to the window*) : I am so very sorry.

EDWARD : He must come soon, mustn't he ?

MELANIE : Yes, he is late now.

EDWARD : I wish that you loved me, really.

MELANIE : So do I.   You would be so easy to love.

EDWARD : Are you unhappy ?

MELANIE : Yes.

EDWARD : Because you love him so much ?

MELANIE : Because he does not love me—enough.

EDWARD : Do you think he ever will ?

MELANIE : Yes.   I know it.

94

EDWARD : I shall remember you always—whatever happens to me.

MELANIE : I will remember you too. I will remember how you put away your own happiness to help me, and even if we see each other again very little, and even when we become very old people, and even when the day comes when I must die, you will be in my heart truly as a kind and dear friend.

" NEVERMORE."   MELANIE.
Verse.

Dear Friend,
If hearts could only be
Content with love and sympathy,
How sweetly we could live,
We both of us have so much love to give.
No matter how our minds conspire,
Imprisoned by our own desire,
We are not free to choose.
What love we gain,
What love we lose,
We cannot choose.

Refrain.

Nevermore.   Nevermore,
Can life be quite the same.
The lights and shadows change,
All the old familiar world is strange,
Evermore.   Evermore,
Our hearts are in the flame.
Others may regain their freedom,
But for you and me,
Never-nevermore.

EDWARD : Melanie !

He takes her in his arms and kisses her. PAUL *enters quietly and sees them. He looks angry for a moment, and then assumes a charming smile.*

PAUL : I hope I am not intruding.

MELANIE (*breaking away*) : Paul !

PAUL : I see that you have returned to reason.

MELANIE : Yes, Paul.

PAUL : I am glad.

MELANIE : Yes, Paul.

PAUL : Lord Sheere, I congratulate you.

EDWARD (*stiffly*) : Thank you.

PAUL : It is so pretty to see Youth—in love.

EDWARD : Love is a very strange sensation, Monsieur le Duc—for Youth, particularly so. When one is young one feels things so strongly. One feels— foolishly perhaps—that the very fact of loving is enough—worth making all sacrifices for. It is sad— almost tragic—to think that with age so much of the best in life loses its savour. You have my sympathy, Monsieur le Duc.

He bows abruptly to both of them and goes out.

PAUL *goes to the writing table.*

PAUL : You should be very happy with him. He seems to be quite suitably unbalanced.

MELANIE : Yes, Paul.

PAUL : You are going to marry him ?

MELANIE : Yes, Paul.

PAUL : I am very glad.

MELANIE : Yes, Paul.

PAUL : But I think it is a little vulgar of you to fall into his arms with such abandon, so soon after the scene you made last night.

MELANIE : Yes, Paul.

PAUL : The game is over now, so you can speak in French if you like.

MELANIE : Oui, Paul.

PAUL (*irritably*) : Qu'est-ce que vous avez ce matin ?

MELANIE : I think I would prefer to talk in English.

PAUL : Pourquoi ?

MELANIE : Because it feels more happy—to-day.

PAUL : You are in love ?

MELANIE : Yes, Paul.

PAUL : So am I.

MELANIE : Oh ! (*She laughs.*)

PAUL : Why do you laugh ?

MELANIE : I thought you would say that.

PAUL : I am going to marry Lady Julia.

MELANIE (*calmly*) : Yes, Paul.

PAUL : Can you say nothing else but " Yes, Paul " ?

MELANIE : There is nothing else to say.

PAUL : The whole thing has been a mistake—a ridiculous horrible mistake.

MELANIE : Yes, Paul.

PAUL : When are you going to be married ?

MELANIE : Soon—very soon.

PAUL : What about money ?

MELANIE : That will not matter. It never does.

PAUL : I will see that you have everything you want.

MELANIE : That is very kind—of Lady Julia.

PAUL : Why do you stare at me like that ?

MELANIE : I am sorry.

PAUL : Have you anything to reproach me with ?

MELANIE : No.

She shrugs her shoulders and walks away.

97

PAUL : Melanie——   (*He goes to her.*)

MELANIE : Yes, Paul.

PAUL : I am sorry—very sorry.

MELANIE : No, no, I am good now—you cannot make me cry.

PAUL : I don't want to make you cry.   I wish with all my heart for you to be happy.

MELANIE : I will be happy then.

  He stirs a cup of chocolate.

PAUL : Will you stay here ?   The rent is paid for six weeks more.

MELANIE : I do not know.

PAUL : I am going to London.

MELANIE : When ?

PAUL : To-morrow.

MELANIE : So soon.

PAUL : But I will come back—in a little while—to make all arrangements for your marriage.

MELANIE : Very well.

PAUL : Does that satisfy you ?   (*He drops a spoon noisily.*)

MELANIE : Yes, Paul.   (*She turns away.*)

PAUL : Please don't look sad.

  She walks away.

MELANIE : It is not real sadness.

PAUL : All comedies must come to an end.

MELANIE (*turning again*) :   I have one thing to ask—it is very small.

PAUL : What is it ?

MELANIE : Come once more to see me before you go.

PAUL : No—no——

MELANIE : Please—it is not much to ask—come this evening to a little supper—I will invite Lady Julia also, and Edward, my fiancé—it will be to celebrate that we are all so happy.

PAUL : C'est un enfantillage.

MELANIE : It will be very gay, and at the same time it will be a little sad—but please, please in memory of our happy days together—please say you will come ?

PAUL : But, Melanie—my dear child——

MELANIE (*very softly*) : Please ?

PAUL : Very well.

MELANIE : Merci, mon cher, cher ami——

 She goes up to him quite simply and kisses him on the mouth.   He instinctively succumbs to her kiss for a moment, and then, breaking away from her abruptly, he goes hurriedly from the room.   She is left standing still for a moment, and then, with an expression of triumph on her face, she runs to the window to see him go.   She begins to sing gaily and a trifle hysterically, and she is still singing as she runs towards her room as the lights fade.

ACT III

SCENE III

The following Scene is cued to music.

> *This Scene is the gardens again. It is evening, and although most of the lights are still shining, there are very few people about. Occasionally a couple stroll across and are lost to sight among the shadows. The orchestra plays softly and sentimentally. Presently* PAUL *enters. He stands looking about him for a moment, as though he were lost. Two lovers cross in front of him, so engrossed in each other that they do not even notice him. He walks slowly down to the bench left. As he is about to sit down upon it, two more lovers pass. They stop still for a moment in a close embrace and then go on their way.* PAUL *sits down disconsolately. Somewhere in the distance* MELANIE'S *voice is heard singing.* PAUL *starts to his feet sharply, and then sinks back again, realising that the voice is only in his mind. The little boy who bowled the hoop in the first scene comes on, but this time his hoop is looped over his left arm while his right encircles the waist of a little girl. They giggle happily across the stage and disappear. The music swells, and with it,* MELANIE'S *voice grows louder.* PAUL *rises with his hands to his ears and starts to move away, but wherever he turns he is met by lovers. The whole scene slides almost imperceptibly into a form of ballet. Finally with all the lovers circling round him and tormenting him, he breaks away and runs off the stage, as the lights fade.*

ACT III

SCENE IV

The Scene is MELANIE'S *room again. The room has been completely dismantled. There are neither curtains, rugs, nor furniture left. The floor is covered with straw and shavings and pieces of rope, all the paraphernalia of packing. The windows are wide open, and strong moonlight floods into the room, which, itself, is lit only by a few meagre candles. The noise of the waves on the shingle can be plainly heard. Arranged round the room are various boxes and trunks and packing cases. At one of these* ROSE *is kneeling, with a pile of clothes on the floor beside her.*

There is a knock on the door.

ROSE (*over her shoulder*): Come in.

 EDWARD *enters. He gives a little start of astonishment.* ROSE *rises to her feet.*

EDWARD: The front door was open, so I came straight——

ROSE: I left it open on purpose, in case I didn't hear.

EDWARD: What has happened?

ROSE: There is a note for you.

EDWARD: Where is Mademoiselle?

ROSE: She has gone.

EDWARD: Gone!

ROSE: The note will explain everything. Here it is.

> *She hands him a note, which is lying on one of the packing cases.*

EDWARD : Thank you. (*He opens it and reads it by the light of one of the candles.*)

> ROSE *resumes her packing.*

EDWARD : Where has she gone ? She doesn't say.

ROSE : France. She left on the evening boat for Dieppe. You can see its lights out there, the sea is calm, so it isn't going very fast.

> *He crosses sadly to the opposite window, looks out, then reverently kisses the note. While he is standing looking out of the window there are footsteps on the stairs and* LADY JULIA *sweeps into the room.*

JULIA : Good Heavens !

EDWARD : I fear that Mademoiselle is not entertaining this evening after all.

JULIA : Obviously.

EDWARD : She has gone.

JULIA : Do you know, I almost gathered that.

ROSE : There is a note for you, Madame.

JULIA : How polite. It would have saved me considerable inconvenience if she had sent it to my house.

ROSE (*curtly*) : Here it is, anyhow.

JULIA (*taking it*) : Thank you.

> *She, too, reads by the light of one of the candles. When she has finished it, she laughs.*

JULIA : Extraordinarily well phrased for a guttersnipe.

EDWARD (*hotly*) : Melanie was not a guttersnipe.

JULIA : I'm so sorry. I had forgotten your great tenderness for her.

EDWARD : I never shall.

JULIA (*smiling*) : Faithful unto death !

EDWARD : Yes. I am her friend, for always.

JULIA : How touching. All the same I cannot help feeling that it is just as well for you that she has gone away.

EDWARD (*turning away*) : I wouldn't expect you to understand, Madame.

JULIA (*loosening her cloak*) : Well, I suppose we had better wait here and break the news to Paul.

ROSE (*still packing*) : That would be waste of time, Madame.

JULIA : Why, what do you mean ?

ROSE : Monsieur le Dook sailed with Mademoiselle on the evening boat for France.

JULIA (*sharply*) : What !

ROSE : You can still see the lights from the window. They look ever so pretty reflected in the water.

JULIA (*furiously*) : You're lying ! Monsieur le Duc couldn't possibly have sailed.

ROSE : That's as may be, but I did happen to see him on to the boat myself. They was very gay—both of them.

JULIA (*controlling herself*) : I see. (*Bitterly.*) How very, very amusing.

ROSE : A joke's a joke all the world over, I always say.

JULIA : Lord Sheere, will you kindly escort me to my house ?

EDWARD : With pleasure, Lady Julia.

JULIA : I fear my cook will be in bed, but I can offer you a little wine.

EDWARD : Thank you.

JULIA : We can drink a toast—to absent friends !

    Without looking at ROSE, *she walks out of the room.*

EDWARD *is about to follow her, then he hesitates and comes back.*

EDWARD : Good-bye, Rose.

ROSE (*jumping to her feet, and curtseying*) : Good-bye, my lord.

EDWARD (*giving her a little purse of money*) : Will you please keep this in remembrance of me ?

ROSE : Oh, yes, my lord—thank you.

He goes to the door and turns.

EDWARD : If—if you should ever see her again—give her my love.

ROSE : Yes, my lord.

EDWARD *goes out.*

ROSE *stands looking after him and after a moment or two she resumes her packing, humming to herself meanwhile. Presently there are hurried footsteps on the stairs and* PAUL *bursts into the room. His face is white, and he is trembling.*

PAUL : Rose ! What's the matter ? What is happening ?

ROSE (*rising to her feet*) : You've missed them, sir.

PAUL : Missed whom ?

ROSE : Lady Julia and Lord Sheere. They just went out.

PAUL : Where is Mademoiselle ? (*He rushes towards the bedroom door.*) Where is Mademoiselle ?

ROSE : You've missed her too, sir.

PAUL : What do you mean ?

ROSE : She has gone.

PAUL : Gone—where—where has she gone ?

ROSE : France, sir—she left a note for you—here it is.

She takes a note from the bosom of her dress and gives it to him. He takes it mechanically, with an expression on his face of utter despair. ROSE *watches him, she starts to*

104

*sing quietly. When he has finished reading it, he walks
slowly across the stage.*

PAUL (*to* ROSE—*stamping his foot*): Stop singing!
(*Speaking with great difficulty.*) She doesn't give any
address—she doesn't say where I can find her——

*He turns slowly round, goes up to the window and
looks out at the sea, then, resting his head on his arms,
he breaks down completely. ROSE looks at him for a
moment, and then slams down the lid of the trunk she
has been packing and walks into the bedroom, her heels
clattering sharply on the bare floor. In a moment or
two her footsteps are heard again, but this time it is
MELANIE who comes out of the bedroom. She clatters
in with the same tread as ROSE. She is dressed for
travelling and carries a paper bag of humbugs in her
hand. She looks at PAUL in indecision for a second,
then she marches across the room and slams down the
lid of another trunk. He does not look round. She
goes to another box and slams down the lid of that.
Still he pays no attention. Finally, when she has
slammed all the lids of all the boxes, she goes quietly
up to him, and sinks on to the floor behind him. She
takes his hand which is hanging down by his side, and
very tenderly kisses it. He turns slowly, and she
proffers him the paper bag.*

MELANIE: Mon cher amour—would you like a
oomboog?

CURTAIN.

105